Speeding Up Microsoft Excel

30 Methods for Improving Calculation Performance

Henrik Schiffner

Users often no longer have to worry about performance and calculation times. That's fine, until they really experience Excel slowing down.

Speeding Up Microsoft Excel

30 Methods for Improving Calculation Performance

ISBN-13: 978-1545075074

ISBN-10: 1545075077

Self-published

professor-excel.com/performance-book

performance@professor-excel.com

Warning and Disclaimer

Contents

Introduction

You are holding a book about improving the speed of Excel calculations, so it's fair to assume that you're struggling with Excel's performance.

Excel is an excellent tool for performing calculations. Just a few years ago, many of the complex calculations you can do today were not even possible or required significant simplifications. You probably won't agree with this while in your current situation, but Microsoft has made some powerful improvements to Excel over the years. These improvements over the last decade have improved data handling and calculation performance. To a certain degree, you can now throw all your raw data into Excel and conduct a large analysis. It is now possible to create very intricate models and conduct complex calculations.

If you've used Excel for a long time—for example, before Excel 2007—then you'll know what I'm talking about. Today, you can solve problems in Excel that were simply impossible because of previous "hard" restrictions, such as only being able to use 65,536 rows.

Because of these improvements in Excel's limitations and calculation capabilities, users often no longer have to worry about performance and calculation times. That's fine, until they really experience Excel slowing down.

Figure 1 shows calculation times and the Excel user's feelings according to those times. Everything below 1/10 of a second for one round of calculation feels instantaneous, and there's no noticeable delay. Between 1/10 of a second and 1 second, the delay is noticeable but still acceptable. It gets annoying for the user when Excel takes longer than 1 second but under 10 seconds; in these cases, the user can still concentrate on the current work stream. For calculation times in excess of 10 seconds, the user usually loses track and shifts his or her concentration to other tasks (1).

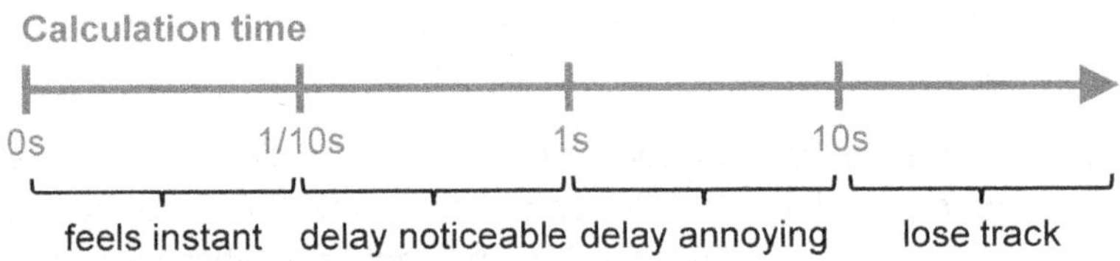

Figure 1: Calculation time and the feeling for an Excel user

The intention of this book is to provide you with quick help when you need it. You will not get a lengthy theoretical discourse here (although the first chapter does start with the theoretical background of Excel's calculation processes) but rather a hands-on recipe for what to do when things slow down.

The problem with improving calculation performance is that every Excel model is different. Therefore, the methods you'll learn in this book will have a different impact depending on your situation. Some of the methods may work very well and help a lot, while others might not help at all. For example, one piece of advice is to switch your computer to an English language region. If your computer is already set to English—for example, "English (United States)"—then you can't gain anything from that tip. If your computer is set to any other language region than English, however, then your calculation time will instantly be reduced by at least 70 percent.

Another annoyance with large Excel files is the long time required to open them. Besides reducing actual calculation times, you'll also get to know a few methods for reducing the time it takes to open an Excel workbook.

In conclusion, this book includes a variety of ways to save you time when working with sophisticated Excel files. Some might work for you, while others might not. But the following pages should provide you with simple guidelines on how to immediately increase the calculation speed and improve the opening performance of your Excel files.

Chapter 1: Theoretical background of Excel's calculation process

With the 2007 version of Excel, Microsoft fixed many workbook and worksheet limitations, for example by increasing the number of rows and columns in a worksheet. Now that these changes have been made, it is necessary to optimize the workbook and the environment for the best possible performance. Fortunately, the newer Excel versions have already become a lot smarter under the hood. The whole calculation process has improved.

It helps a lot to understand what Excel is doing in the background. Although the methods for improving calculation performance discussed later concentrate on specific actions, it is worth spending a little time on the theory first.

Principles of calculation in Excel

You might find yourself stuck in a long calculation at this very moment, so the following sentences might sound a little off to you. But Excel is already quite smart; the newer version of Microsoft Excel can handle complex calculations relatively well.

Excel only calculates the changes in your workbook. Sounds simple, right? It is—and it isn't. How does Excel know which cells to calculate? Figure 2 shows the three steps of the calculation process in Excel. The steps will be explained in detail on the following pages.

Figure 2: The calculation process in Excel

Step 1: Build the initial calculation chain

When you open an Excel workbook, it builds the initial calculation chain. Roughly speaking, the calculation chain[1] tells Excel which cells depend on which other cells and in which order they should be calculated. That means that Excel does not have a fixed order for the calculation process—for example, from top to bottom or from left to right. Instead, one global calculation chain exists for the whole workbook. (In pre-2002 versions of Excel, the program had separate calculation chains for each worksheet.)

---

[1] To keep things simple, the dependency tree and the calculation chain will be summarized under the term "calculation chain". Strictly speaking, Excel constructs the calculation chain from the list of dependencies (cell B depends on A, and so on), which is called the calculation tree.

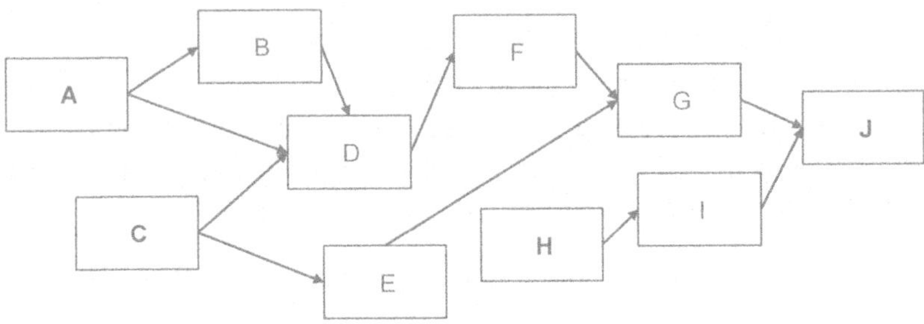

Figure 3: Example of a calculation chain

Figure 3 shows an example of a calculation chain, assuming that cells A, C, and H are input cells with no preceding cell. All these cells lead through calculations in other cells (for example, in cells B, D, and E) to cell J. Cell J has no dependent cell. With a few exceptions, any calculation will be conducted along this chain.

Step 2: Track dependencies

Excel users don't usually notice the second step of the whole calculation process, in which Excel permanently updates the calculation chain. It also tracks if a cell remains uncalculated. This happens even in manual-calculation mode. In this context, the uncalculated cell is also called a "dirty" cell (2).

Back to the sample calculation chain. If you change cell A, then Excel not only has to recalculate cell A, but it also has to recalculate cells B, D, F, G, and J, as shown in figure 4. Before the actual calculation is conducted, Excel only marks these cells as dirty so that they will eventually be recalculated; all the other cells, meanwhile, will not require recalculation.

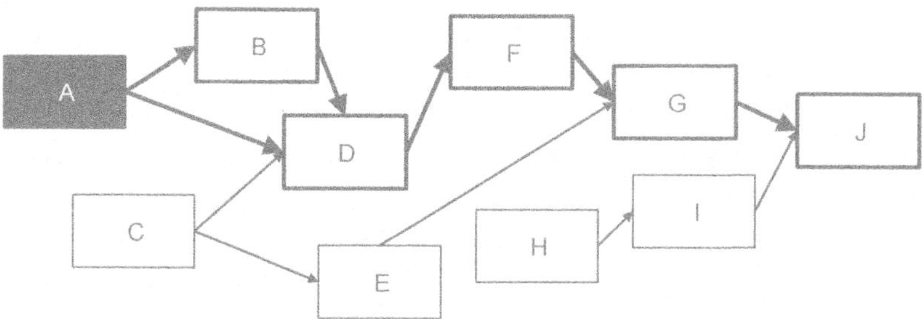

Figure 4: Calculation chain for a change in cell A

As is so often the case in life, every rule has an exception, and this rule is no different. Please bear the following exceptions in mind.

- *Volatile formulas.* Volatile formulas will be recalculated each time Excel calculates, no matter if changes have been made. These formulas are:
  - RAND()
  - NOW()
  - TODAY()
  - OFFSET()
  - CELL()
  - INDIRECT()
  - INFO()
- *User-defined volatile formulas.* Such formulas are programmed in a VBA (Visual Basic for Applications) macro and are used in your workbook.

Step 3: Calculate formulas

Excel eventually starts the actual calculations of the cell values. But Excel now only calculates the dirty cells to keep the calculation time low. You might notice that Excel gets faster the second time it calculates. This could be because of the following reasons.

- The number of dirty cells is often reduced. Once the workbook is finished calculating and there are no more changes, Excel will not calculate these cells again.
- Excel refines the calculation chain for future calculations during the calculation process. It gets smarter. For example, it is possible that a cell can get calculated more than once at the beginning, because Excel might notice that another preceding cell has changed. The second time Excel calculates, the program adapts the sequence and calculates all preceding cells first.
- The first calculation has resulted in improvements of some kind; for example, Excel stores often-used values more efficiently and uses computer resources better (1).

When you experience slow performance, the slowness usually originates from this third step of the calculation process. This is also the step where you have the highest influence on.

Calculation modes

In the previous chapter, you learned how Excel sets up and calculates the calculation chain. The next important question is: How can you gain from that knowledge? Fortunately, there's good news. Excel allows you to take control of both *when* and *what* to calculate.

Moment of calculation

Imagine this situation. You have a large Excel file, and the calculation is taking longer than 1 minute. You don't want Excel to perform calculations every time you enter data or a formula, do you? In automatic calculation mode, Excel starts a recalculation after each of the following triggers:

- pressing Enter when editing a cell;
- changing a cell, for example by copying and pasting values or using in-cell drop-down lists;
- pressing F9, Shift + F9, or Ctrl + Alt + F9;
- changing filters, for example setting or removing a filter;
- changing PivotTables;
- inserting or deleting rows, columns, or cells;
- renaming or reordering worksheets;
- filtering, hiding, or unhiding rows;
- opening or saving a workbook.

In some cases, you might not notice the calculation because the cell you changed was not part of a calculation chain. You can also easily interrupt calculations: even moving the mouse might stop a calculation, which will proceed once you stop moving the mouse. The only "stable" method of calculation is to save your file. When you save your file, Excel calculates your workbook. This calculation can only be interrupted by pressing Esc on the keyboard.

You can set Excel to calculate only when you want it to calculate. To do this, switch to manual-calculation mode.

1. Go to the "Formulas" ribbon and click on "Calculation Options."
2. Three options are available, as shown in figure 5: "Automatic," "Automatic Except for Data Tables," and "Manual."

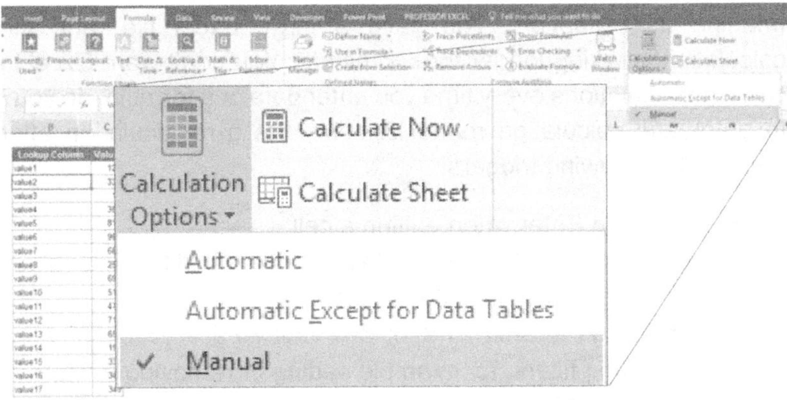

Figure 5: Switching to manual-calculation mode in Excel

"Automatic" and "Automatic Except for Data Tables" are quite similar. The only difference is that besides the formulas, automatic mode permanently recalculates data tables, whereas "Automatic Except for Data Tables" mode ignores data tables.[2]

---

[2] A data table is a range of cells that simulates a calculation result if two input variables change. The data table is part of Excel's "What-If" analysis features. The structured data format (sometimes also referred to as a data

But what does automatic calculation mean? Broadly speaking, it means that Excel calculates all open workbooks every time you change something. (See the list of triggers for a calculation on page 15.) Manual calculation means that Excel only calculates when you ask it to recalculate. You must actively initiate the calculation process. How do you initiate a recalculation, you might ask? Here's how:

- if you press F9 on the keyboard
- if you click on "Calculate Now" on the "Formulas" ribbon
- if you save an Excel file (it will then also be recalculated)

Scope of calculation

In manual-calculation mode, you can select which part of your Excel workbook should be recalculated.

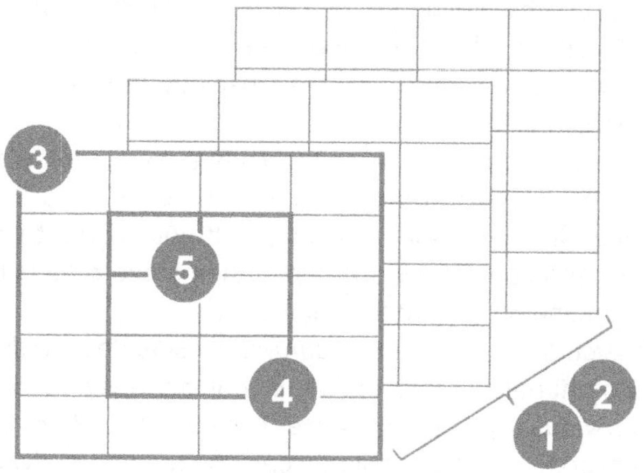

Figure 6: Decide which parts of your workbook should be calculated

---

table) is not intended in this context. For more information about data tables, please refer to page 39.

Figure 6 and the list below show the five basic options of the scope of a calculation.

1. *All formulas in all open workbooks, whether they're calculated or not.* For such a so-called full calculation, press Ctrl + Alt + F9 on the keyboard.
   Recommendation: Start a full calculation if you have the feeling that some of the formulas are not showing the correct results. Especially in very large Excel workbooks or with many cancelled calculations, the underlying calculation chain or cell flagging might be damaged. By pressing Ctrl + Alt + F9, you can "repair" the chain.
   Please note that a full calculation usually takes significantly longer than just the "normal" calculation (the second item of this list below), which only regards all uncalculated cells.
2. *All open workbooks.* To improve performance, this "normal" calculation only considers all uncalculated dirty cells. Press F9 on the keyboard or go to "Formulas" and click on "Calculate Now." Please keep in mind that any other workbooks open in the background will also be recalculated.
3. *Alternatively, you can only calculate the current worksheet.* In the manual mode, press Shift + F9, or go to "Formulas" and click on "Calculate Sheet." If your current worksheet depends on other worksheets, then those cells in the other worksheets will not be calculated.
4. *Calculate only the currently selected cell range.* Unfortunately, this option is not as easy to do as the previous options, because there's no built-in button or keyboard shortcut, but you can use a comparatively simple VBA code by following these steps:
   a. Select the cells that you want to be calculated.
   b. Press Alt + F11 on the keyboard; the Visual Basic editor should now be open.

      c.   Press Ctrl + G on the keyboard. The immediate window within the Visual Basic editor will open.

      d.   Copy and paste in or type in this code:

```
Selection.Calculate
```

      e.   Press Enter on the keyboard.

5.   *One cell only.* Enter a cell, for example by pressing F2 on the keyboard or by double clicking on the cell. Press Enter on the keyboard to leave the cell. If you are in manual-calculation mode, then only this cell will be recalculated.

In addition to these five options, you can further decide if data tables should be recalculated.[3] Go to "Formulas," click on "Calculation Options" and select "Automatic Except for Data Tables."

Summary of calculation modes

Excel allows you to take control of when and what part of your workbook to calculate. The following table summarizes the available calculation options in the manual and automatic calculation modes.

---

[3] For more information about data tables, please refer to page 39.

Table 1: Overview of calculation modes

Calculation scope	Calculation mode "Manual"	Calculation mode "Automatic"
All formulas in all open workbooks	Press Ctrl + Shift + F9	Press Ctrl + Shift + F9
All changes in all open workbook	Press F9 or go to "Formulas" and click on "Calculate Now"	Not selectable in automatic mode
Worksheet	Press Shift + F9 or go to "Formulas" and click on "Calculate Sheet"	Not selectable in automatic mode
Selection of cells	Use VBA macro `Selection.Calculate` in the immediate window of the Visual Basic editor (please refer to page 18 for more information)	Not selectable in automatic mode
Single cell	Enter the cell (F2 on the keyboard) and press Enter on the keyboard	Not selectable in automatic mode

Recommendation: in most situations, you'll do fine by remembering the following three points from this chapter:

- If Excel becomes slow, then switch to manual-calculation mode.
- You can recalculate everything by pressing F9.
- You can recalculate just the current sheet by pressing Shift + F9.

Chapter 2: Improve calculation performance

In the previous chapter, you learned the basics of various Excel calculation processes. Now it's time to use that knowledge while exploring 30 hands-on methods for speeding up Excel calculations.

Structure of each method

Each of the following methods can lead to a performance improvement of some kind. Each is introduced by three parts:

1. *Idea*. The basic concept of the method is outlined within a few sentences; this part contains a summary of the theory behind a given method.
2. *Implementation*. This is a step-by-step guide for you to implement the method; this part allows you to easily apply a method even if you don't know all the theoretical background. Most methods include a numbered list of steps. These numbers usually relate to numbers on a screenshot, which will make it easier for you to follow the steps.

   One word of caution: when you apply the steps to your own Excel model, please save your work before or between steps. Some of the methods described in this book require major changes to your workbook or system.

3. *Impact.* Before you implement any method, you should make sure that you (and your workbook) will really gain from it. The reduction of calculation time (in percentages) is shown for each method. For example, please see figure 7; if the full calculation required 100 seconds before the method was applied and 10 seconds after, then the reduction is 90 percent. This percentage should provide a rough impression of whether it is worth it for you to spend the effort in improving the calculation time.

A VBA macro (page 123) was used to test the impact of the various methods. The macro runs six full calculation rounds and determines the calculation times for each round. In order to make the results comparable, the first, slowest, and fastest rounds were removed from the results.

The test workbook has a simple structure. The base version has 100,000 VLOOKUP formulas and 10,000 data sets. For some tests (for example, to measure the impact of array formulas), the workbook was adapted to meet the test requirements.

Please note that each percentage shown applies only for that particular test workbook and environment. The actual impact for your workbook will be highly dependent on your own situation: your Excel workbook and computer environment. This value provides a fairly rough indication of possible improvements you can make.

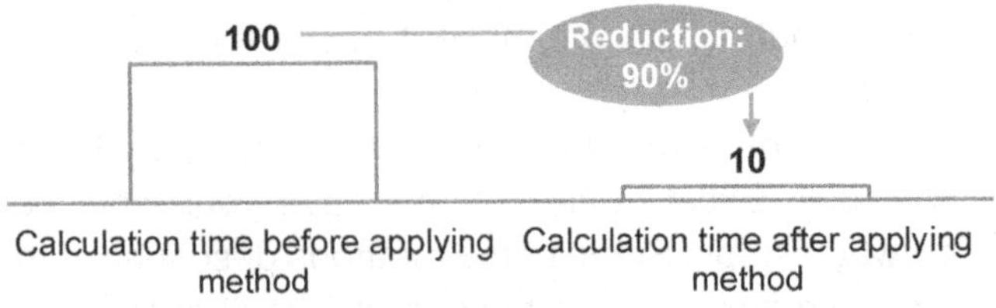

Figure 7: Example of a reduced calculation time of 90 percent

30 methods for improving calculation performance

In this chapter, you'll learn 30 selected methods for speeding up Excel. The list of methods has been compiled from several different sources, including

- recommendations from Microsoft's Excel team;
- available advice on the internet;[4]
- information derived from the study "Performance of Excel: Study Shows How to Speed Up Excel by 81%" (3);
- analyses and experience of the author.

The 30 methods can be divided into four groups, defined by the effort required to implement each method and the reduction of calculation time that's possible. Figure 8 shows all the methods as well as the methods' classification into the four groups.[5] The numbers in the chart refer to the number of the method in this chapter.

- Group 1 (the "Quick wins" group) contains all methods that are easy to implement and that may significantly reduce calculation times.
- The methods in group 2 are also effective, but they usually require more effort to implement than those in group 1. This is the "Difficult but effective" group.
- The effects of the methods in group 3 are often limited (at most a 12 percent performance reduction) but are usually easy to implement. This is the "Worth a try" group.

---

[4] A lot of advice is available online, although some of the methods available often have little to no impact on the calculation time. A few of the most common methods are still listed in this book in order to provide a recommendation *not* to use them.
[5] Please refer to page 123 for the complete list of methods.

- The methods within group 4 usually require a lot of effort, and the performance improvement is at most 15 percent. In other words, you don't get much bang for your buck. This is the "Last resort" group.

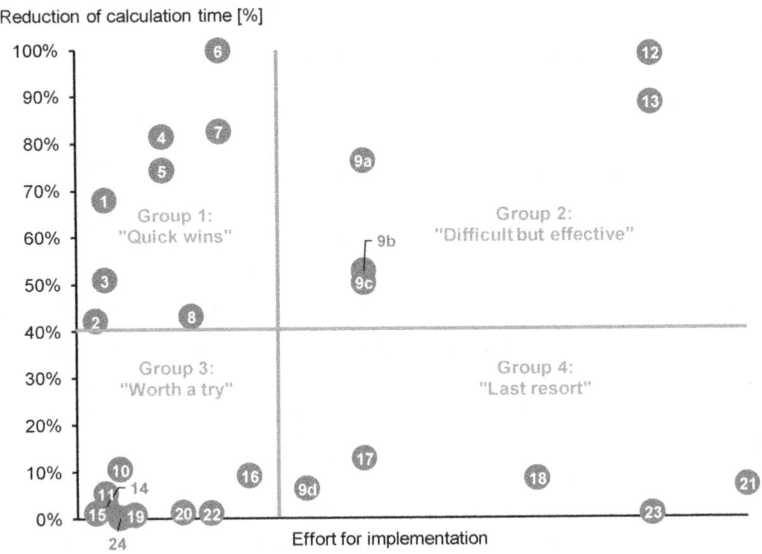

Figure 8: Overview of the various methods for speeding up Excel calculations[6]

As described on page 21, the reduction of calculation time (on the vertical y-axis shown in figure 8) was measured with a VBA macro. The effort for the implementation of a method (the horizontal x-axis)

---

[6] Methods 25 through 30 are not included in the overview due to their negative (or not measurable) impact.

is based on experience and a rough estimation; there is no scientific background to that number.

The 30 methods in this chapter are arranged in the following order: by the reduction of calculation time (in percentages) divided by estimated effort (in seconds). For example, because hypothetical method A reduces the calculation time by 50 percent and requires 200 seconds for implementation, while method B reduces the calculation time by 40 percent but only requires 100 seconds, method B will be listed ahead of method A.

01. Avoid links to other workbooks, or keep linked workbooks open

Idea

Links to other Excel workbooks (also called external references) are sometimes unavoidable but often come with more disadvantages than advantages: they are slow and difficult to find, they break easily, and they are often simply annoying. (You've probably experienced the error message when opening a workbook with external links in which Excel asks you if you'd like to refresh the linked data.)

Implementation

You have various options for handling external links in Excel. The easiest method is to break all links. Please note that all formula cells with references to other workbooks will be replaced by values.

1. Click on "Edit Links" on the "Data" ribbon. If the button is grayed out and you can't click on it, then your workbook does not have external links, and you can stop here.
2. Select the link that you want to break. Again, a word of caution: please be aware that your calculation might be damaged and may not work as it did before. Also, links can't be restored once they're broken.
3. Click on "Break Link."

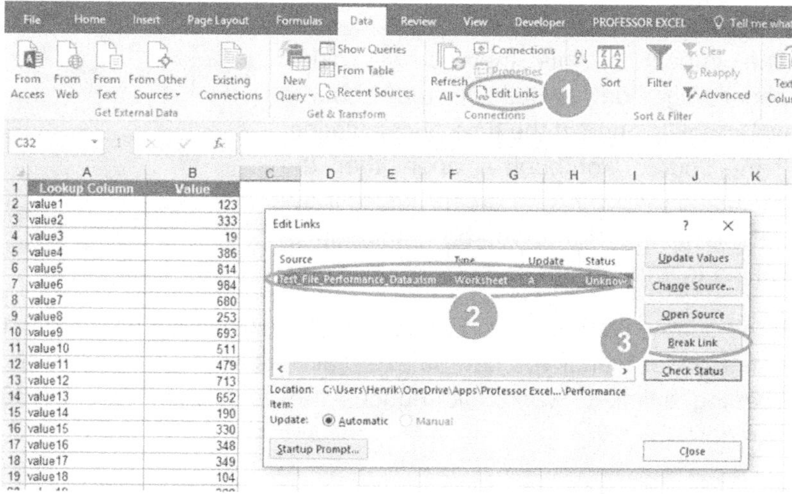

Figure 9: Steps for breaking workbook links

You also have a few other options. If you want to maintain references to other workbooks instead of breaking them, please consider the following options.

- Keeping the linked workbook open when Excel performs calculations can significantly speed the calculation process (as long as your source workbook does not require calculations to be performed).
- Use direct cell links, for example

  `=[Source_WB.xlsx]Sheet1!A1` instead of formulas that refer to ranges in the other file, such as

  `=VLOOKUP(A1,[Source_WB.xlsx]Sheet1!A:B,2,FALSE)`.
- Consider alternative methods, for example using queries to retrieve data from the other workbook.

Impact

The impact of this method will differ, depending on whether the source workbook is open at the time of calculation. If the source workbook is open, then the calculation will be 0.7 percent faster if the data is in the same workbook instead of linking to another open workbook.

Reduction of calculation time:

68%

If the source workbook is closed, then the calculation will take 3.1 times longer than if you had no external links at all. In other words, opening a linked workbook reduces the calculation time by 68 percent.

02. Use all available processors for calculations

Idea

Modern computers usually have more than one processor. Excel can use this situation to split calculations across several processors and calculate (for example) one thread on each processor.[7]

There are some restrictions, though:

- You will only experience improvements in calculation performance if your workbook has more than one independent calculation tree. A workbook with more than one calculation tree "will show gains close to the number of processors available," according to Williams, Bokone, and Rothschiller (4).
- Some features do not support multithreaded calculations, including
  - data-table calculations
  - user-defined functions
  - XLM functions
  - the INDIRECT, CELL, and GETPIVOTDATA formulas
  - the VBA functions `Range.Calculate` and `Range.CalculateRowMajorOrder`
  - circular-reference loops

The default setting is that Excel will use all available processors, but once your workbook has been calculated and saved with fewer processors, Excel usually stays with the lower number of processors.

---

[7] A thread is the "smallest sequence of programmed instructions that can be managed independently," according to *Wikipedia* (10).

Implementation

The implementation is quite simple (see figure 10):

1. Click on "Home" and then "Options."
2. Click on "Advanced" on the left-hand side.
3. Scroll down until you reach the "Formulas" section.
4. Make sure "Enable multi-threaded calculation" is checked.
5. Now you have two options:[8]
    a. "Use all processors on this computer" (recommended) or
    b. Set the number of threads manually.
6. Confirm with "OK."

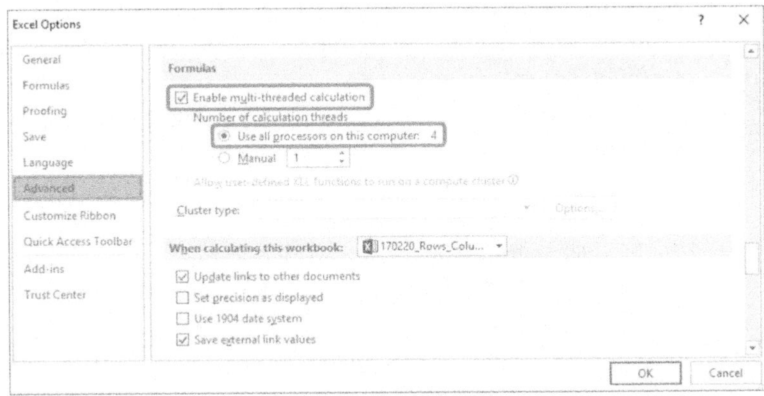

Figure 10: Enable multi-threaded calculations

---

[8] For step 5 above, you must differentiate between the number of threads and the number of processors. The number of processors is equal to the number of cores of your computer, while a thread is just a virtual sequence; one processor can host more than one thread. You can set the number of threads manually to a maximum of 1,024 threads in Excel. *Recommendation*: The option "Use all processors on this computer" is usually a safe choice, but you can—and you are encouraged to—test what happens if you manually change the number of threads.

Impact

The effect with a test workbook is quite clear: changing the number of processors from four processors to one processor increases the calculation time between 62 and 94 percent. Alternatively, switching from one processor to four processors reduces the calculation time by from 39 to 49 percent.[9]

Reduction of calculation time:

39% to 49%

---

[9] The test was done under three different environments and settings, which led to this range of performance increases (3).

03. Close other workbooks in the background

Idea

Excel calculates all open workbooks. That means that other workbooks in the background will also consume computing performance. But this situation only counts for workbooks with cells that are flagged as uncalculated and that have volatile formulas such as INDIRECT or OFFSET (please refer to page 12 for more information). If you initiate a full calculation (see page 17) with multiple workbooks open, however, then Excel's performance will suffer.

Implementation

Close any other open workbooks by activating them (for example by pressing Alt + Tab on the keyboard until the other workbook is displayed). Then close the other workbook by pressing Alt + F4, or alternatively go to "File" and click on "Close." Save your work first if necessary.

Impact

The effect of closing other workbooks is of course highly dependent on the performance requirements of the other workbooks. A test using the same workbook that was opened twice in different versions showed the expected result: a full calculation took twice the time.

Reduction of calculation time:

51%

There is one exception when using this method, which is in cases where you have external links to the other workbook in the background. In such cases, it is often faster to leave the linked workbook open. Please refer to the method "Avoid links to other workbooks, or keep linked workbooks open" on page 26 for more information.

04. Switch the Windows region to "English (United States)"

Idea

Modern hardware and software environments (your computer and the operating system, Windows) are built for the English language system. They can of course handle other languages, but they are optimized for English input, processing, and output.

A member of the Microsoft Excel team has explained it this rather technical way: "The reason is that we can short-circuit English to byte comparison. More complex scripts require involving more heavy Unicode machinery" (5).

The concept is to set your computer's language region to English: for example, to "English (United States)."

Implementation

Probably the fastest way to implement this is to follow these steps.

1. In Windows 8 or 10, press the Windows key and start typing "region."
2. If your search result shows the "Region" settings within the Control Panel, as shown in figure 11, then press Enter.
3. Change "Format" to "English (United States)." Any other English region, such as "English (United Kingdom)," is also fine.
4. Optional: Adjust the date and time settings per your own language and preferences.
5. Confirm with "OK."

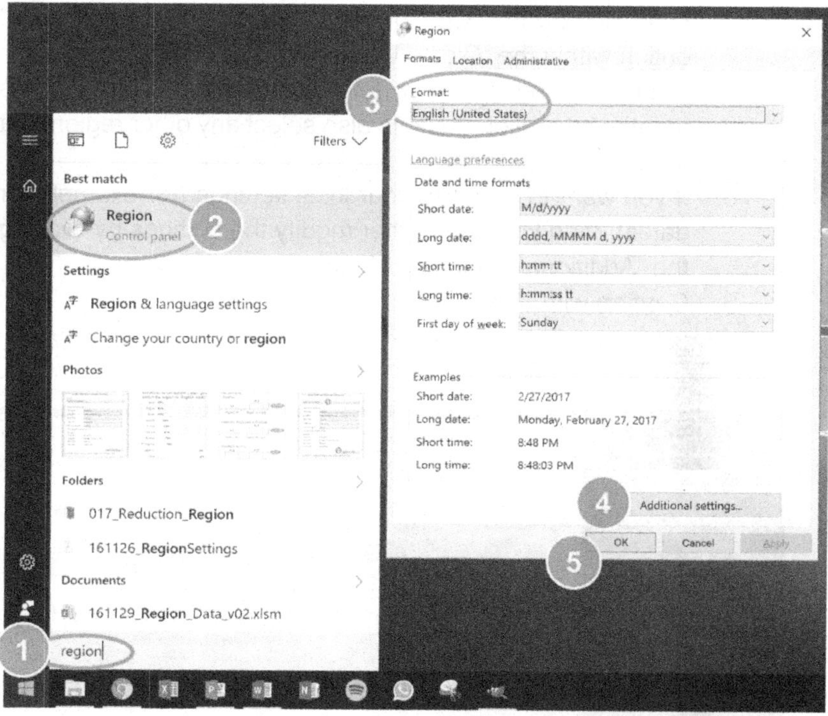

Figure 11: Steps for changing the computer's region (first method)

Another way to change the region settings is to open the Control Panel.

1. Right-click on the Start button in the bottom left corner of the screen (in Windows 8 or 10). In Windows 7, click on "Start" and then on "Control Panel."
2. Open the Control Panel.
3. If the view of the Control Panel is set to "Small icons" or "Large icons" (as shown in figure 12), then just click on "Region." If your Control Panel is organized by "Category,"

> then click on the "Change date, time, or number formats" option within the "Clock, Language, and Region" group.

4. Change "Format" to "English (United States)." As mentioned earlier, you can also select any other region that starts with "English."

5. If you want to return to your local settings (for example for dates), then you can further modify the settings by clicking the "Additional settings…" button.

6. Confirm with "OK."

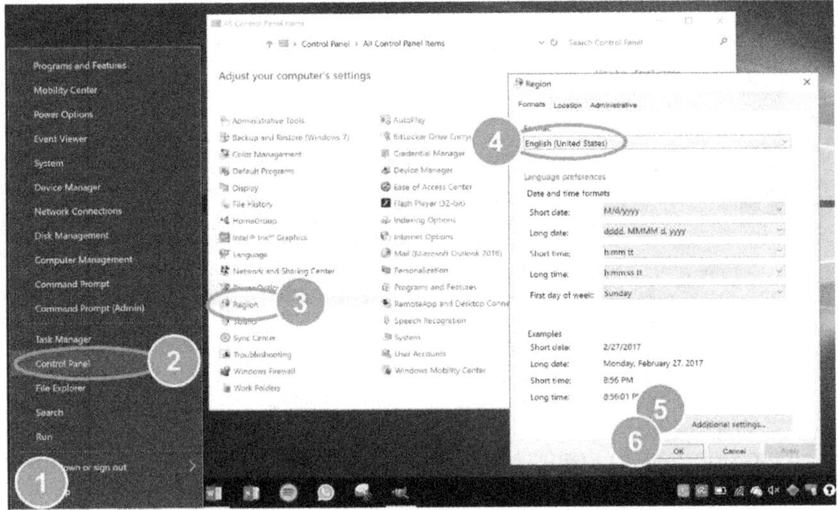

Figure 12: Steps for changing the computer's region (second method)

Please note that you should not change the *language* of your computer or of Excel. Only the *language region* as shown before of the computer matters.

Impact

If you change the language region of your computer to any "English" language region, then the impact will be very high. With a simple test file containing 50,000 VLOOKUP formulas, the effect was significant, as shown in figure 13. The results ranged from an 82 to 99 percent reduction of calculation times.

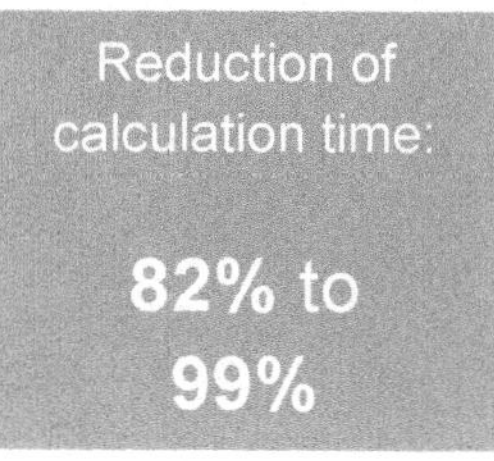

The different language regions can be summarized in four different groups:

1. The first group is the reference region, "English."
2. The second group contains a group of highly heterogeneous regions with markedly different languages, including Chinese, Greek, Korean, German, Japanese, and Russian. By changing the region from one of these languages to English, you can reduce calculation times by at least 82 percent.
3. The third group required 12 to 23 times the amount of time to calculate a test file compared to using English, which means that you can reduce calculation times by from 92 to 96 percent by making this switch. Somewhat surprisingly, this group contains "Spanish," but "Portuguese" is listed in group 2.
4. The fourth group required from 44 to 70 times the calculation time than was the case with English. In terms of reduction, this means that you can reduce calculation times by almost 99 percent if you switch from one of these languages (Hindi, Punjabi, or Bangla, for instance) to English (6).

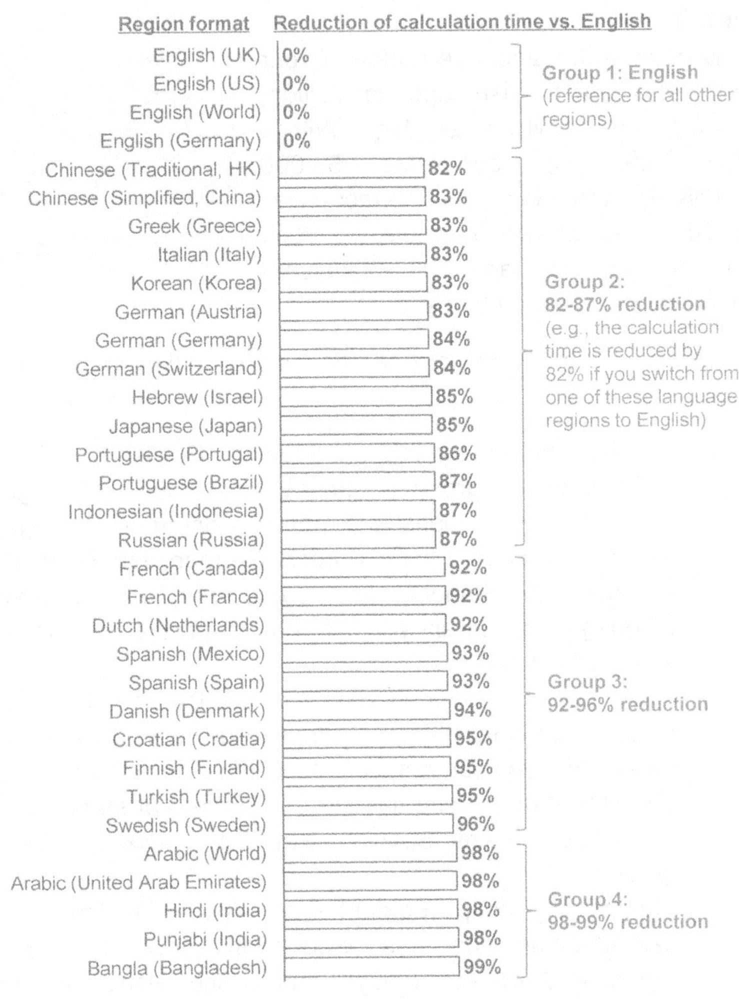

Figure 13: Reduction in calculation times for a simple test file after changing the computer's language region settings[10]

---

[10] The values represent the reduction of the calculation time (in percentages) compared to the English reference region (group 1). Your

05. Minimize using data tables or skip calculating data tables

Idea

Data tables are a great way to simulate different scenarios. You can change two input variables at the same time and let Excel simulate the whole calculation for each combination of these two variables.

Gross profit (USD)

		Price					
		7.00 USD	8.00 USD	9.00 USD	10.00 USD	11.00 USD	12.00 USD
Amount sold	80	-220	-140	-60	20	100	180
	90	-210	-120	-30	60	150	240
	100	-200	-100	0	100	200	300
	110	-190	-80	30	140	250	360
	120	-180	-60	60	180	300	420

Figure 14: Example of a data table

Figure 14 shows an example of a data table. The columns simulate different prices (from 7 to 12 USD), and the rows contain amounts sold, from 80 to 120 units. The numbers in the center of the data table run through a calculation chain and represent the gross profit for each combination of price and amount.

The problem is that each calculation round takes time. If you have five different values for each variable, then Excel must conduct your calculation 25 times.

---

actual values may vary from the results shown here, depending on your workbook and computer environment.

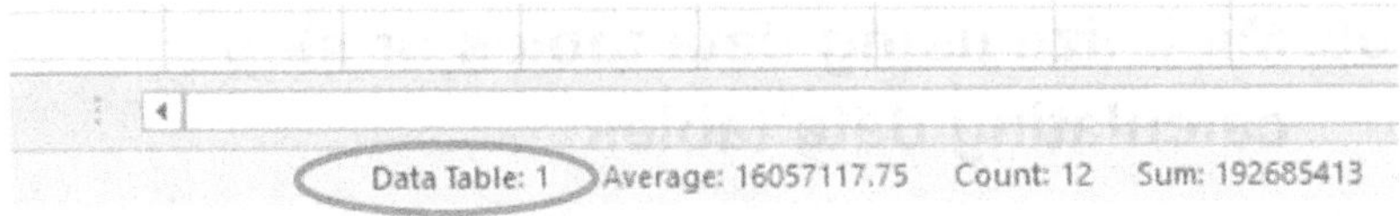

Figure 15: When Excel calculates data tables, it will show the current number of the data table in the status bar

Implementation

When Excel calculates data tables, it is written "Data Table: 1" (or any other number in the status bar, as shown in figure 15). The number is the current number of the data table that Excel is calculating at that moment.

There are two approaches for handling data tables:

1. avoid data tables, and only use them if necessary;
2. because Excel provides a setting in which data tables are not recalculated every time Excel does a calculation, you can go to "Formulas" and click on "Calculation Options." Switch to "Automatic Except for Data Tables." (See figure 16.)

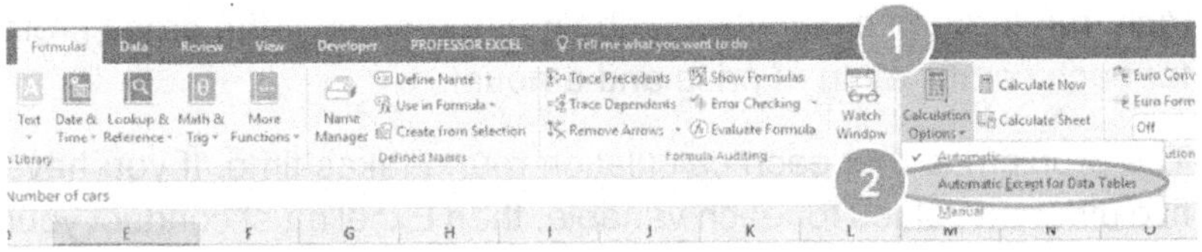

Figure 16: Changing the calculation mode to "Automatic Except for Data Tables"

Impact

The calculation time can be reduced by at least 50 percent with this method.[11] But again, it is highly dependent on your workbook and the following variables.

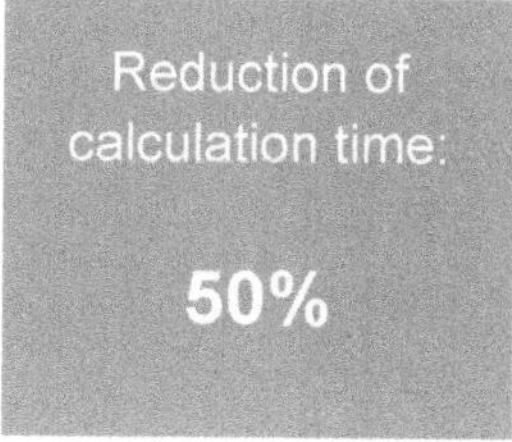

- *Number of data tables*. How many data tables are you using?
- *Size of the data tables*. How many scenarios are your data tables calculating?
- *Calculation time for one calculation*. How long does one calculation round take?

Or, to put it in mathematical terms:

$$Calculation\ time = \sum_{DT=1}^{n} rows_{DT} \times columns_{DT} \times t_{DT} + t$$

where n = the total number of data tables, DT = the data table, and t = the time for one calculation.

Thus, the calculation time for a simple test workbook increases almost linearly. The vertical axis in figure 17 shows the calculation time, while the horizontal axis shows the number of data table cells in the workbook.

Figure 17 indicates that each data table has a fixed amount of calculation time per data table. It also appears as if even numbers of cells require slightly more time than odd numbers of cells, although there does seem to be a linear relation (as assumed) between the number of cells in the data tables and the calculation time.

---

[11] The performance improvement of 50 percent is the minimum improvement, calculated if you have the smallest possible data table in your workbook (one data table with a size of 1 x 1 cells).

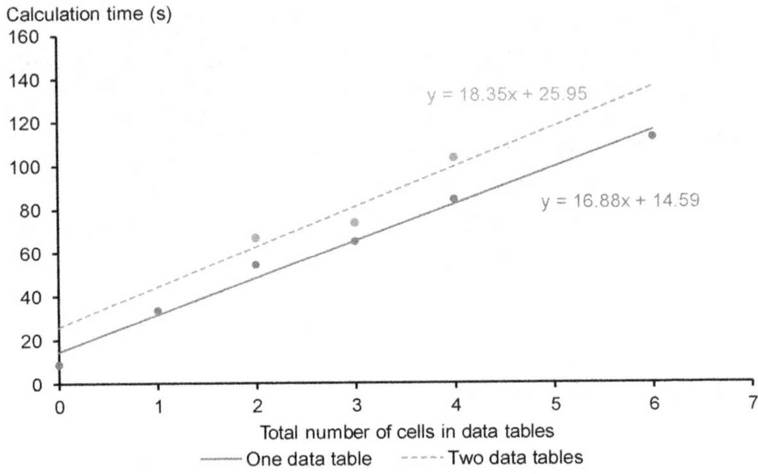

Figure 17: The calculation time of an Excel workbook that includes data tables correlates to the total number of cells in the data tables

06. Array formulas 1: Use the exact range in array formulas

Idea

Array formulas extend normal formulas.[12] According to Mike "excelisfun" Girvin, they "can replace intermediate steps and provide single cell solutions" (7). As an example, the VLOOKUP formula does not allow multiple search criteria: you can only search for one value at a time, or use a workaround (for example by inserting a helper column). Alternatively, array formulas can achieve multiple search criteria in a VLOOKUP formula without using a helper column.

As you can see from the following example, array formulas can be very useful. After typing an array formula into an Excel cell, you must press Ctrl + Shift + Enter instead of just Enter.[13] By pressing Ctrl + Shift + Enter, Excel adds the curly brackets { and } that enclose the formula.

Array formulas generally have one major disadvantage: they are comparatively slow to calculate. If you use an array formula—which you may want to avoid in terms of calculation performance (please see page 56)—then make sure that you refer to the exact cell range instead of entire columns. Normal formulas today can handle larger areas of unused cells very well—unused cells are simply omitted during the calculation process—but array formulas cannot.

Because array formulas play an important part in advanced Excel modeling, this book includes two recommendations for array formulas: use the exact cell reference in array formulas, or avoid them in general (please see page 56).

---

[12] An array is a range of at least two or more cells.
[13] They are also referred to as CSE (Control, Shift, Enter) formulas.

Implementation

Instead of referring to complete columns in array formulas, just use the exact cell range you need for the formula. Here are two examples.

1. Instead of A:A, refer to A1:A100 (assuming that's your relevant cell range).
2. In terms of array formulas, instead of using the formula[14]

```
{=VLOOKUP(A2&B2,CHOOSE({1,2},LookupValues!$A:$A&Lo
okupValues!$B:$B,LookupValues!$C:$C),2,0)}
```

refer to the exact cell range:

```
=VLOOKUP(A2&B2,CHOOSE({1,2},LookupValues!$A$2:$A$1
001&LookupValues!$B$2:$B$1001,LookupValues!$C$2:$C
$1001),2,0)
```

Impact

The impact of reducing the cell reference in array formulas to the actual range you are using is very high. With the formulas above (example 2), the reduction of calculation times by changing entire columns to exact cell ranges in the formulas is approximately 99.7 percent.

Reduction of calculation time:

99.7%

---

[14] The array formula in this example achieves a multi-conditional VLOOKUP without using an additional helper column.

07. Solve circular references and reduce iterations

Idea

Simply speaking, a circular reference occurs when cell A refers to cell B, and cell B refers to cell A. But often, circular references not only regard two cells, but also follow a long chain of cells. These circular references can slow down the calculation process. The basic idea of this method is to avoid circular references in general. If you want to maintain them, then try to reduce the maximum number of iterations, since each iteration takes time to be calculated.

Implementation

Excel offers two helpful functions concerning circular references. It helps you find circular references, and you can let Excel solve circular references with iterative calculations.

To find circular references, follow these steps to identify and remove them.

1. Go to the "Formulas" ribbon.
2. If the "Formula Auditing" group is collapsed, as shown in figure 18, then click on it. Otherwise, just continue to step 3.
3. Click on "Error Checking."
4. If the "Circular References" button is grayed out such that you cannot click on it, then your workbook has no circular references. If it is not grayed out, then your file has circular references.

5. After clicking on the "Circular References" button, you'll see a list of cells that are involved in the circular reference. This list could potentially contain hundreds of cells.

6. When you enter a formula that turns out to be part of a circular reference, Excel warns you with an error message. It also shows you the circular reference, with blue arrows pointing out the calculation chain for the circular reference.[15]

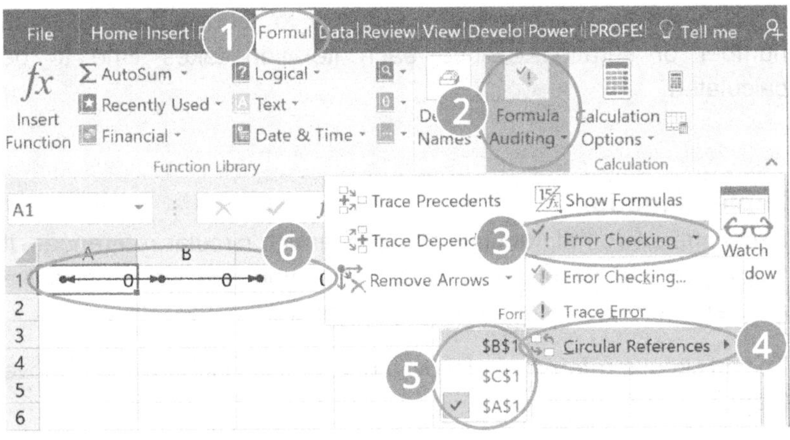

Figure 18: Steps for identifying circular references

People often don't intentionally create circular references; instead, they usually result from formula errors. To remove unintentionally created circular references, you'll need to correct the corresponding formulas. Here's a simple example. If cell A refers to cell B, and cell

---

[15] You can remove the blue arrows that show circular references by clicking on "Remove Arrows" in the "Formula Auditing" section of the "Formulas" ribbon.

B refers to cell A, then you must break the circle, for example by making cell B refer to cell C instead of cell A.

Alternatively, you can replace one formula cell of the circle by using hard values. Copy and paste one of the cells by using the "Paste Special" dialogue (press Ctrl + Alt + V on the keyboard). Select "Values" and press Enter.

In some cases, you will want to keep the circular references and allow Excel to iterate in order to calculate the result. Excel 2016 allows up to 32,767 iterations. To do this, follow these steps.

1. Click on "File" and then "Options." Navigate to "Formulas," as shown in figure 19.
2. Check the box "Enable iterative calculation." You can further set the maximum number of iterations as well as the maximum change at which you want Excel to stop iterating. The default value is 100 iterations.

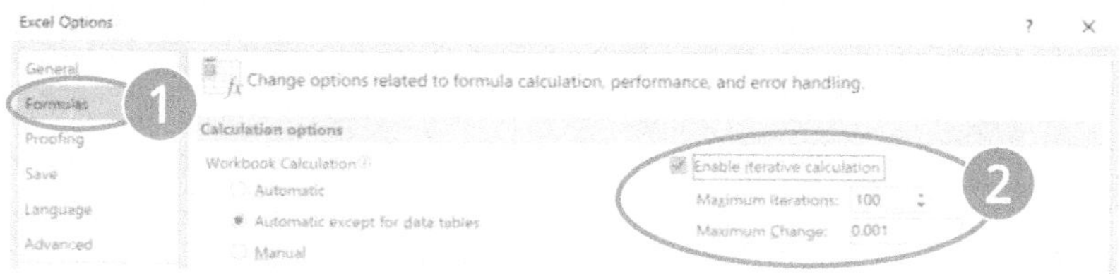

Figure 19: Enable iterative calculation and set the maximum number of iterations

When Excel calculates iterations, you can see the status bar in the bottom-right corner of the screen, which displays the number of the current iteration (for example, "Itr: 1"). In most cases, the maximum number (100 in this case) will not be reached, because the change is smaller than your defined maximum. In practice, if the maximum number of 100 iterations is reached, then the iteration process is stuck and will not yield better results. You can (carefully) reduce the number and see if the results worsen.

Impact

A test file with two sets of 5,000 VLOOKUPS that referred to each other showed a significant impact on the calculation performance. Removing the circular references but keeping the same amount of VLOOKUP formulas reduced the calculation time by 82 percent.

Reduction of calculation time:

82%

If your Excel workbook has a similar quantity of circular references, then you can achieve similar reductions in calculation times. If you only have one or two circular references, however, then the impact on calculation performance by removing them will not be particularly high. You should still consider solving these references, though.

08. Avoid large used ranges in formulas

Idea

Method 6, "Array formulas 1: Use the exact range in array formulas," already dealt with overly large ranges in formulas. But method 6 focused on array formulas, which always calculate the complete range in formulas, regardless of whether the range has any contents.

But normal formulas—that is, not array formulas—can handle overly large ranges in formulas quite well. They determine the actual so-called "used range"[16] and only regard that range, even if the cell reference in the formulas is larger than the range. For example, if only rows 2 through 20 have data, then Excel only regards and calculates the formula `=SUM(C:D)` as `=SUM(C2:D20)`.

The problem is that Excel sometimes fails to determine the actual used range especially with older versions of Excel (2003 and older). Later releases of Excel may also regard overly large ranges and thus require more calculation time.

Implementation

The used range in formulas may be reduced in two ways.

1. Adapt the cell references in formulas so that they apply to the relevant cell range.
2. Reduce the used range on worksheets.

---

[16] According to Microsoft, "a used range includes any cell that has ever been used. For example, if cell A1 contains a value, and then you delete the value, then cell A1 is considered used". (12)

Option 1: Adapt the cell reference in formulas

Applying the first option is easy, but it does require some effort, as you must edit frequently complex formulas. First, change the cell-range reference within your formulas to the smallest possible range. As an example, instead of `=SUMIFS(A:A,B:B,X1)`, you could write `=SUMIFS($A$3:$A$120,$B$3:$B$120,X1)` if your lookup table only stretches across the range A3–B120.

Please note the following comments.

- If you refer to the exact range instead of entire columns (or rows), then the formulas will become longer and more difficult to read and debug. The example above illustrates this quite well.
- When you add data to your table (for example, a new row 121), don't forget to update the range to $A$3:$A$121.
- Add the $ signs for fixing the cell range. In this way, the range will not be adapted when you copy and paste the formula.

Option 2: Reduce the used range on worksheets

The second option is to reduce the used ranges on worksheets. This option comprises two steps: identifying the used range and then changing that range.

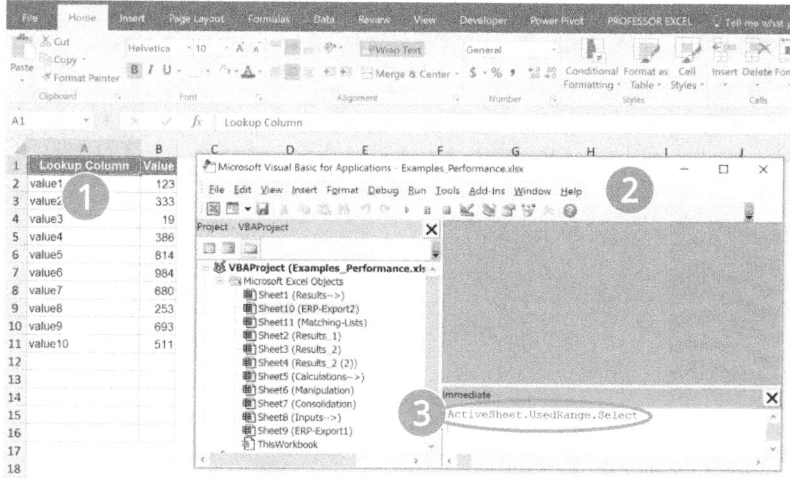

Figure 20: Identifying the used range

The first step in identifying the used range (see figure 20) involves the following steps.

1. Select any cell on your current worksheet.
2. Open the Visual Basic Editor by pressing Alt + F11 on the keyboard.
3. Go to the immediate window (by pressing Ctrl + G on the keyboard) and paste in the following code:
   ```
   ActiveSheet.UsedRange.Select
   ```
   Press Enter, and the used range on your current worksheet will be selected.

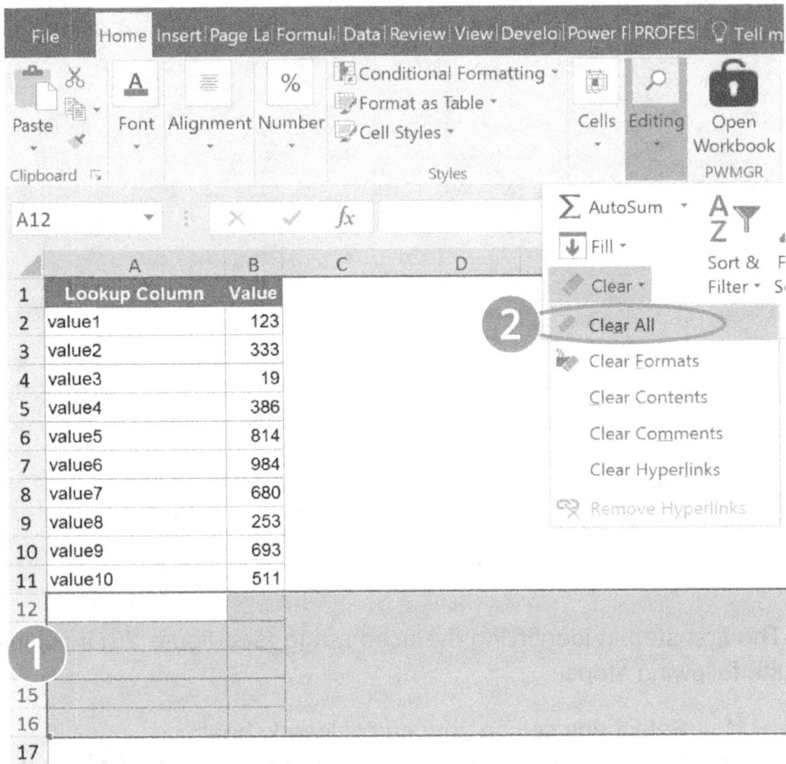

Figure 21: Reducing the used range you're using to that of your actual data

The second step is to reduce the used range. If the used range is larger than that of your actual data, then you should reduce the range by following these steps.

1. Select the cells that are larger than your actual data but still within the used range. In figure 21, this is rows 12–16.
2. Click on "Clear" within the "Editing" group on the "Home" ribbon. Then click on "Clear All."

You can now check to see if the reduction of the used range works by repeating the first step, as described on the previous page.

Impact

Excel usually recognizes the correct cell range as the used range and only regards the cells in that range for calculations. In these cases, you can't save much calculation time by further trying to adapt formulas or used ranges. The test showed only a 1 percent reduction of calculation times.

Reduction of calculation time:

1% to 43%

If the used range is much larger than the range that has actual content, then the increase in performance could be significant. For testing purposes, the lookup data was located much lower down on the worksheet (between rows 100,000 and 110,000 instead of between rows 1 and row 10,000). In these cases, you can save roughly 43 percent on calculation times if you move the data up to rows 1–100 on your worksheet.

As mentioned before, there is one exception to this rule, which is when you use array formulas; in these cases, you should always use exact cell references, because Excel does not recognize used ranges but instead regards all cells in the given cell ranges. Please refer to pages 43 and 69 for more information on array formulas.

09. Use faster formulas

Idea

All roads lead to Rome. For many calculations, there's more than one way to accomplish the calculation. Some formulas require longer calculation times, while others are faster. Before jumping right in with the distinct formulas, here's some general advice.

1. Start optimizing the formulas you use multiple times. If you use a formula just once or twice, then it's usually not worth spending time on it.
2. A general rule of thumb is to start with the longer formulas—lookups, for example. Such formulas might use longer absolute calculation times and thus have higher potential to improve overall calculation speeds. Exceptions abound, of course.
3. Measure the impact. A stopwatch might be possible, or you could use a VBA macro. Please feel free to use the VBA macro shown on page 122.

Implementation and impact

Table 2: Selected Excel formulas and their faster alternatives

Formula	Description	Impact
A2+B1 instead of SUM(A$1:A2)	If you accumulate numbers, don't use the formula SUM(A$1:A2) and copy it down. Refer to the last value above, and just add the new value with A2+B1 instead.	76%
IFERROR instead of IF(ISERROR)	The IFERROR formula is much faster than the long IF(ISERROR) formula combination.	50%
INDEX/MATCH instead of SUMIFS	If you use the SUMIFS formula for a simple lookup, consider using INDEX/MATCH instead. VLOOKUP is slightly slower than VLOOKUP but is also a possible alternative formula.	47%
MAX(A1,0) instead of IF(A1>0,A1,0).	=MAX(A1,0) is about 6% faster than =IF(A1>0,A1,0). But please note that both formulas are very fast, so it's highly unlikely that this is your calculation's bottleneck.	6%
INDEX/MATCH instead of VLOOKUP	As mentioned before, the INDEX/MATCH formula combination is slightly faster than VLOOKUP.	1%

The formulas listed above are just a few examples. The total improvement to calculation performance will depend on whether these formulas really are the bottleneck. For instance, the formula `=MAX(A1,0)` is faster than `=IF(A1>0,A1,0)`. But calculating both formulas is very fast in terms of absolute numbers. In most cases, replacing the formula will not improve your performance significantly unless you use it thousands of times in your workbook.

10. Sort data for lookups

Idea

Excel calculates things faster if your data is sorted. This is especially true for lookups, for example a VLOOKUP formula or INDEX/MATCH. The concept of this method is thus to sort the lookup data by search column, in ascending order.

Implementation

Because your data is usually organized vertically, the following example focuses on vertical sorting for now.

1. Select the data you wish to sort.
2. Click on "Sort" in the center of the "Data" ribbon.
3. Select the first column to be sorted. In this case, it is the first column of your lookup range, as the lookup will search through this column. The order should be "A to Z," or "Smallest to Largest" for numeric values.
4. Confirm with "OK."
5. If your data is organized horizontally, then click on "Options" before clicking "OK." You can then define the sorting direction.

Please note that references to cells that are in different rows within the sorted cell range could be lost or damaged during the sorting process.

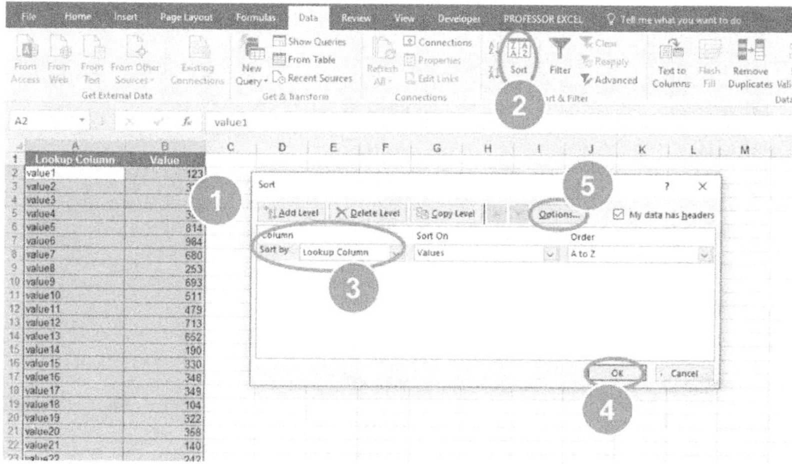

Figure 22: Sorting the data for lookups

Impact

According to Microsoft, "Lookups on sorted data can be tens or hundreds of times more efficient than lookups on unsorted data" (1). A test with alphabetically sorted data did not show performance improvement of "tens or hundreds of times," but there was still some improvement: the test workbook, which had 100,000 VLOOKUP formulas, required 5 percent less time for a full calculation than was the case with unsorted data.

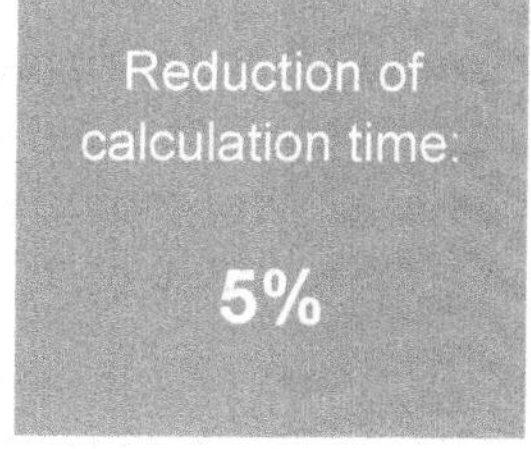

Please take a look at figure 22 again. Column A contains text that says "value1," "value2," and so on. You can sort these values in two ways: alphabetically, or by the trailing number.

Table 3: Comparison of sorting methods

Method 1: Alphabetically	Method 2: Sort by the trailing number
value1	value1
value10	value2
value100	value3
value1000	value4
value10000	value5
value1001	value6
value1002	value7
value1003	value8
value1004	value9
value1005	value10
value1006	value11
value1007	value12
...	...

As noted above, alphabetical (A–Z) sorting leads to 5 percent lower calculation times, but if you can manage to sort the data numerically (as in sorting method 2), then the performance improvement you see could be up to 10 percent.

11. Use the XLSB file type

Idea

XLSB files store data a little bit differently than the XLSX or XLSM file types: they do not use the XLM file structure. Instead, XLSB files save disk space, because the data is stored in the binary structure. The difference is that binary files are computer-readable but not human-readable (8).

The main disadvantage of XLSB files is that binary Excel files can contain VBA macros. If you don't know the origin of a file, please consider its trustworthiness before opening it. For most Excel users, the other disadvantages seem minor.

Table 4 summarizes the advantages and disadvantages of the XLSB format compared to the standard XSLX file format.

XLSB files have a significantly smaller file size than XLSX files, and opening them is much faster (see "The XLSB file type" method on page 107). Also, calculation speeds are a little bit faster.

Table 4: Advantages and disadvantages of the XLSB file format compared to the XLSX file format

Advantages	Disadvantages
<ul><li>Smaller file size.</li><li>Faster opening and closing of files.</li><li>Formulas with more than 8192 characters allowed.</li><li>Can use all the functions available in Excel.</li><li>Faster calculations.</li></ul>	<ul><li>Security: Files can contain VBA code, whereas XLSX files cannot.</li><li>You can't change the Excel ribbon.</li><li>Some third-party tools (e.g., OpenOffice) might not be able to open your file.</li><li>You can't open your files with Excel 2003 or earlier (which today should no longer be a problem).</li><li>Not very well known. Some people might get confused if you send them XLSB files.</li></ul>

Implementation

For changing the default Excel file format "XLSX" to the binary format "XLSB," use the "Save as" function in Excel.

- Click on "File" next to the "Home" ribbon.
- Click on "Save As" on the left-hand side.
- On the bottom of the "Save As" window, change the drop-down field "Save as type" from XLSX to XLSB, as shown in figure 23.

Figure 23: Changing the file format of your Excel file to XLSB

Impact

The calculation of an XLSB file is around 5 percent faster than XLSX, but what's more important about the XLSB format is that the file size is approximately 27 percent lower—although this depends on the content of your workbook—and the opening time is 69 percent lower; see page 107 for more information.

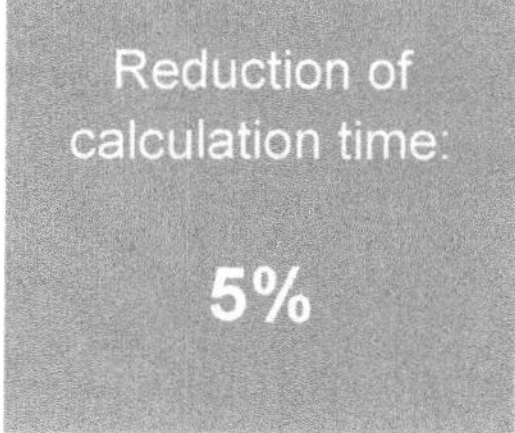

12. "Approximate" and "not exact" matches in lookups

Idea

Excel has two major lookup formulas or formula combinations: VLOOKUP and INDEX/MATCH. Both formulas offer an exact match as well as an approximate match. The advantage of approximate matches is that they are significantly faster than exact matches. Even two approximate matches are much faster than one exact match. You can use this in combination with the IF formula to speed up calculations.

Implementation of the VLOOKUP formula

Admittedly, the implementation is a little bit complicated. The first example we'll cover relates to the VLOOKUP formula. The structure is shown in figure 24. The concept is to use the IF formula and determine if the approximate VLOOKUP can find your search value, which is shown in the first row of figure 24. If the approximate VLOOKUP can find your search value, then you should do an approximate VLOOKUP. If your search value can't be found, then you should do an exact VLOOKUP (the last row of figure 24).

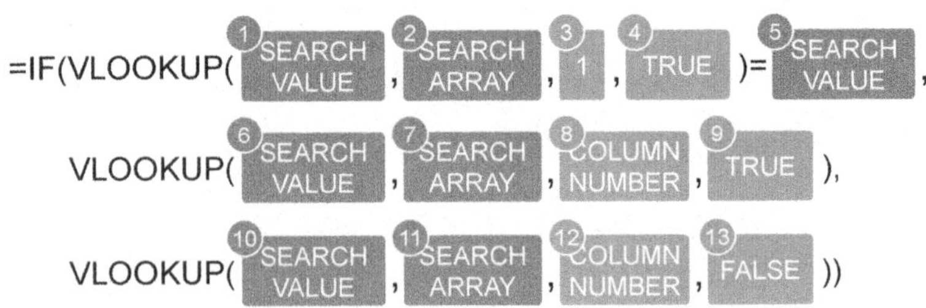

Figure 24: Structure of the implementation of an approximate VLOOKUP

Before jumping right in with the 13 parts of the approximate VLOOKUP formula (as shown in figure 24), please sort the data in the lookup column in ascending order. Although the formula will still deliver correct results, the approximate VLOOKUP only works on data that's sorted in ascending order. For that reason, Excel will not need to draw on the exact lookup in the last row of the long formula shown in figure 24, and it will run much faster.

1. You'll need to include the search value several times. Number 1 is your search value in the first VLOOKUP formula, which checks if your search value can be located with the approximate VLOOKUP.

2. Number 2 is the search array. VLOOKUP searches in the leftmost column of your search array. Because you only check to see if your search value can be found in the search column, the search area can also be reduced to the leftmost column.

3. The return column is also the search column: the first VLOOKUP should return the search value, once the value has been found. This means that the column number is 1.

4. TRUE means that you perform an approximate search.

5. If the result of the VLOOKUP equals the search value, then it is possible to do an approximate VLOOKUP.

6. The second VLOOKUP (the middle row in figure 24) returns the approximate result. Again, use the search value for the approximate lookup.

7. The search array of your second VLOOKUP must contain the search column, which is the leftmost column (the same as item 2 above) and the return column.

8. Which column do you want to be returned? Start counting with your search column as number 1. If you search in column A and want to return a value from column B, then the column number is 2.

9. Again, use the approximate VLOOKUP. To achieve this, you must write TRUE or omit this part of the second VLOOKUP formula.
10. The final VLOOKUP will be used in case the approximate VLOOKUP attempted before doesn't work. Use the same search value again.
11. For the search array, use the same cell range as in item 7 above.
12. The return column also equals the second VLOOKUP (item 8 above).
13. Now you can use an exact VLOOKUP by setting the final part of the third VLOOKUP formula to FALSE.

After knowing the theoretical background, you can proceed to a simple example, as follows. Say you want to replace the exact VLOOKUP formula shown in figure 25 by an approximate VLOOKUP formula. The original, exact VLOOKUP formula is:

```
=VLOOKUP(A2,LookupValues!A:B,2,FALSE)
```

	A	B	C	D	E	
1	Value	Value 2				
2	value1	=VLOOKUP(A2,LookupValues!A:B,2,FALSE)				
3	value2	333				
4	value3	19				

Figure 25: Example of replacing an exact VLOOKUP formula with an approximate VLOOKUP formula

You'll then have the following specifications:

- the search value is cell "A2"
- the search area is "LookupValues!A:B."

- the return value is shown in column B

After putting this information into the structure according to figure 24, you'll then have the following formula:

```
=IF(VLOOKUP(A2,LookupValues!A:B,1,TRUE)=A2,VLOOKUP(A2,
LookupValues!A:B,2,TRUE),VLOOKUP(A2,LookupValues!A:B,2,
FALSE))
```

Implementation of the INDEX/MATCH formula combination

The approximate lookup formula works in a similar way to the INDEX/MATCH formula combination. The basic structure is the same. Using an IF formula, check whether an approximate MATCH is possible; if yes, go with the approximate INDEX/MATCH. If an approximate MATCH is not possible, then use the exact MATCH.

The structure of an approximate INDEX/MATCH is shown in figure 26.

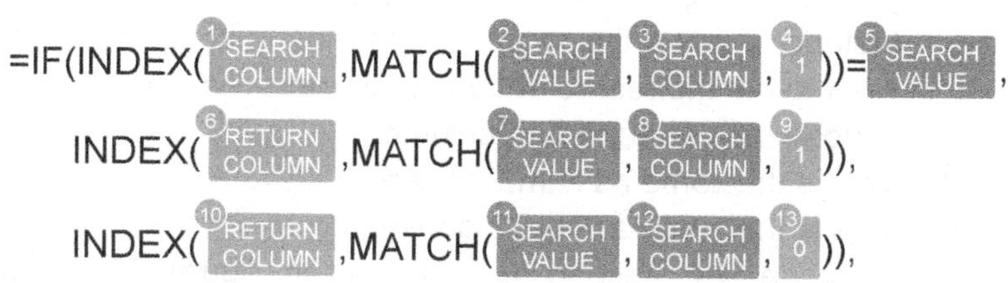

Figure 26: Structure of the implementation of an approximate INDEX/MATCH

1. The INDEX/MATCH formula combination starts with the INDEX formula and its first argument, the return column. Use the search column itself. That way, you're searching

within the search column; once the approximate result is found, you'll also get the result returned from the search column. You can then compare to see if the value found matches with the value you searched for.

2. In all three INDEX/MATCH formulas, the search value is the first argument of the MATCH formulas.

3. Also, the search column—as the second argument of the MATCH formulas—is always the same.

4. The last argument of the MATCH formula determines the type of match:

    a. −1 finds the smallest value that is greater than or equal to your search value.

    b. 0 finds only exact matches.

    c. 1 finds the largest value that is less than or equal to your search value.

Please note that if you choose 1, then your search column must be sorted in ascending order; if you choose −1, then the search column must be sorted in descending order.

5. Compare the return value of the first INDEX/MATCH formula combination to the search value. If it is equal, then you can proceed with an approximate lookup.

6. Instead of using the search column as in item 1, you now want to get the real return value. For this reason, you must choose the correct return column.

7. This is the same as item 2 above.

8. This is the same as item 3 above.

9. Because the second row shown in figure 26 is the approximate lookup, choose either 1 if your search column is sorted in ascending order, or choose 2 if your search column is sorted in descending order. It must be the same as listed in item 4 above.

10. The last INDEX/MATCH formula combination will only be used if an approximate match cannot be found. The formula is therefore almost the same as that shown in the second

row of figure 26. The first argument of this INDEX formula is again the return column, as in item 6.

11. This is the same as item 2 above.

12. This is the same as item 3 above.

13. Item 13 contains the only difference from the second INDEX/MATCH formula: you make Excel search for the exact value by writing 0.

As an example, say you want to replace the exact INDEX/MATCH formula shown in figure 27 with an approximate INDEX/MATCH formula.

◢	A	B	C	D	E	F	G
1	**Value**	**Value 2**					
2	value1	=INDEX(LookupValues!B:B,MATCH(A2,LookupValues!A:A,0))					
3	value2	333					
4	value3	19					

Figure 27: Example of an approximate INDEX/MATCH

This means that the return column is LookupValues!B:B, the search value is A2, and the search column is LookupValues!A:A. If you put that into the structure of figure 26, you'll get this formula:

```
=IF(INDEX(LookupValues!A:A,MATCH(A2,LookupValues!A:A,1))=
A2,
INDEX(LookupValues!B:B,MATCH(A2,LookupValues!A:A,1)),
INDEX(LookupValues!B:B,MATCH(A2,LookupValues!A:A,0)))
```

Impact

The impact depends on how many lookup formulas and how many other formulas you have in your workbook. A test with an Excel workbook that contained 100,000 VLOOKUP formulas and no other formulas had a reduced calculation time of 97 percent. The result using INDEX/MATCH formulas was very similar: the calculation time could be reduced by 96 percent.

13. Array formulas 2: Avoid array formulas

Idea

On page 43, the first method for speeding Excel up introduced array formulas and recommended using the exact cell reference instead of entire rows or columns. The problem with array formulas is that they consume a lot of calculation performance. Because most operations can also be achieved with conventional formulas, helper columns, or other workarounds, you should completely avoid array formulas in terms of calculation efficiency.

Implementation

Most operations can also be achieved with normal formulas by using separate, multiple calculation steps. The application is highly individual, though, because each array formula requires a different approach when you're replacing it with a normal formula.

As an example, if you'll look at figure 28, you'll see that you have a multi-conditional VLOOKUP—in this case a VLOOKUP with two conditions. The data is located on the sheet "LookupValues" in the cell range A2–B1001. The values you search for are shown in cells A2 and B2.

Without going into too many details about how the formula works, the complete array formula looks like this:

```
{=VLOOKUP(A2&B2,CHOOSE({1,2},LookupValues!$A$2:$A$1001&LookupValues!$B$2:$B$1001,LookupValues!$C$2:$C$1001),2,0)}
```

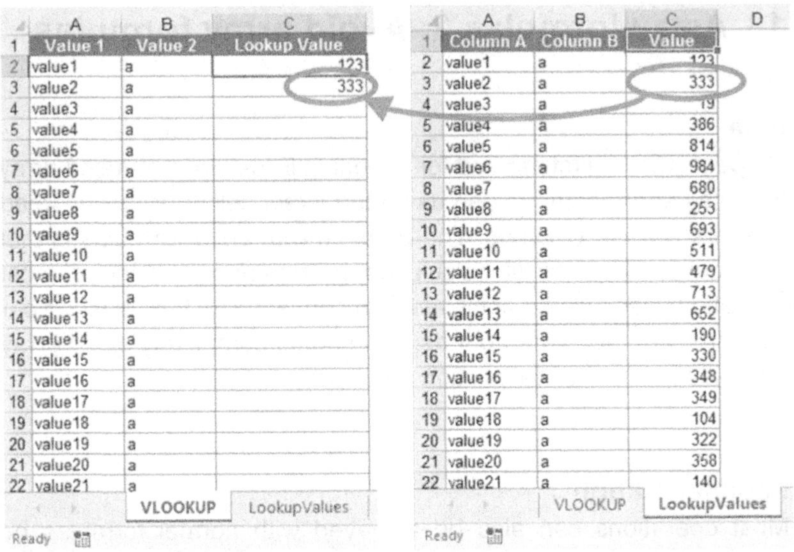

VLOOKUP sheet

	Value 1	Value 2	Lookup Value
1	Value 1	Value 2	Lookup Value
2	value1	a	123
3	value2	a	333
4	value3	a	
5	value4	a	
6	value5	a	
7	value6	a	
8	value7	a	
9	value8	a	
10	value9	a	
11	value10	a	
12	value11	a	
13	value12	a	
14	value13	a	
15	value14	a	
16	value15	a	
17	value16	a	
18	value17	a	
19	value18	a	
20	value19	a	
21	value20	a	
22	value21	a	

LookupValues sheet

	Column A	Column B	Value
1	Column A	Column B	Value
2	value1	a	123
3	value2	a	333
4	value3	a	19
5	value4	a	386
6	value5	a	814
7	value6	a	984
8	value7	a	680
9	value8	a	253
10	value9	a	693
11	value10	a	511
12	value11	a	479
13	value12	a	713
14	value13	a	652
15	value14	a	190
16	value15	a	330
17	value16	a	348
18	value17	a	349
19	value18	a	104
20	value19	a	322
21	value20	a	358
22	value21	a	140

Figure 28: Example of replacing array formulas

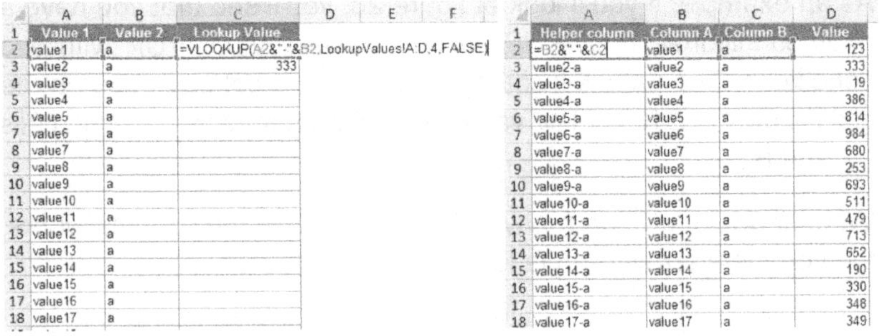

VLOOKUP sheet

	Value 1	Value 2	Lookup Value
1	Value 1	Value 2	Lookup Value
2	value1	a	=VLOOKUP(A2&"-"&B2,LookupValues!A:D,4,FALSE)
3	value2	a	333
4	value3	a	
5	value4	a	
6	value5	a	
7	value6	a	
8	value7	a	
9	value8	a	
10	value9	a	
11	value10	a	
12	value11	a	
13	value12	a	
14	value13	a	
15	value14	a	
16	value15	a	
17	value16	a	
18	value17	a	

LookupValues sheet

	Helper column	Column A	Column B	Value
1	Helper column	Column A	Column B	Value
2	=B2&"-"&C2	value1	a	123
3	value2-a	value2	a	333
4	value3-a	value3	a	19
5	value4-a	value4	a	386
6	value5-a	value5	a	814
7	value6-a	value6	a	984
8	value7-a	value7	a	680
9	value8-a	value8	a	253
10	value9-a	value9	a	693
11	value10-a	value10	a	511
12	value11-a	value11	a	479
13	value12-a	value12	a	713
14	value13-a	value13	a	652
15	value14-a	value14	a	190
16	value15-a	value15	a	330
17	value16-a	value16	a	348
18	value17-a	value17	a	349

Figure 29: One possible method for avoiding array formulas is to instead use helper columns

A multi-conditional lookup can also be conducted by inserting a helper column on the left-hand side of the lookup data. The helper column contains a new primary key, which combines the two lookup columns.[17] In this example, you can see the new primary key in the helper column on the right-hand side of figure 29, in column A. The formula in cell A2 is =B2&C2. Now you can set up a normal VLOOKUP search for the combination of column A and B in the worksheet VLOOKUP.[18]

Impact

As with most cases, the impact of this method will vary depending on your formulas and your Excel environment.

Reduction of calculation time:

88%

In this example, avoiding array formulas and replacing them with a helper column and a new primary key resulted in a reduced calculation time of 88 percent. Please note that the exact cell range was used in the array formula, and not entire columns.

---

[17] The main feature of a primary key is that it is unique for each data set.
[18] Please note that if you use a helper column for a lookup with multiple search criteria, please make sure that the new primary key is actually unique and doesn't exist multiple times. For example, say you have the two data sets "value1"&"22" and "value12"&"2." If they were combined in a new primary key, then both would say "value122." Separating both cells with an additional character could help—for example, by adding a space character or any other separator—but that is not necessarily a safe solution.

14. Set "realtime" priority for Excel in the Windows Task Manager

Idea

In the Windows Task Manager, you can set the priority of the processes that are currently running. The default priority is "Normal," and the possible choices are "Low," "Below normal," "Normal," "Above normal," "High," and the highest value, "Realtime."

Implementation

Changing the priority of a software program in Windows is simple and does not require many steps; the only condition is that the program must already be running. In this case, start Excel first. Next time you start Excel again, you'll have to repeat the following steps.

1. Open the Task Manager by right-clicking on a free part of the task bar at the bottom of the screen.
2. Click on "Task Manager."
3. Once you're in the Task Manager, navigate to "Details." If you only see a very small window without any tabs or details, then click on "More details."
4. Right-click on "EXCEL.EXE."
5. Move the mouse to "Set priority."
6. Click on "Realtime."

Please note that Windows shows a warning message when changing the priority of processes: "Changing the priority of certain processes could cause system instability." Although the test that was run did not reveal any problems, please make sure that you permanently save a backup of your file(s).

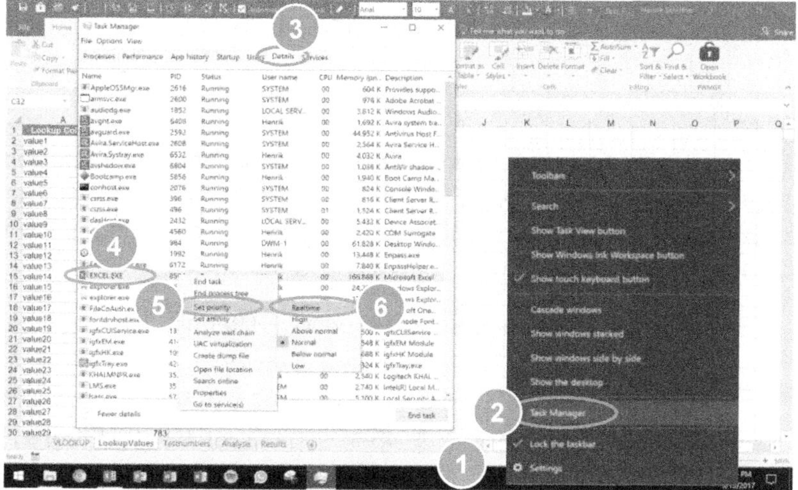

Figure 30: Setting Excel's priority to "Realtime" in the Windows Task Manager

Impact

The impact of changing the process priority from "Normal" to "Realtime" (the highest value possible) led to reduced calculation times of 3 percent in tests.

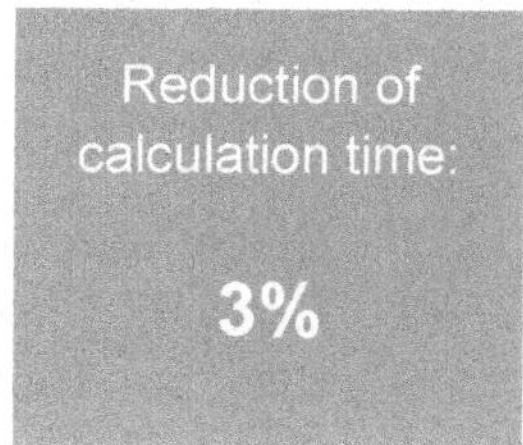

15. Use the Excel table format for data

Idea

Excel has a function called an Excel table (also sometimes referred to as a data table).[19] An Excel table offers a structured way to organize your data. In short, it has a few advantages and disadvantages compared to normal cell ranges.

- A data table offers some built-in filtering, sorting, row shading, and so on.
- By default, a data table uses the same formula for the whole column. It therefore is not possible to use a different formula in a single cell within the data table.

The interesting question is this: Does the Excel table format make Excel calculate more quickly? Let's find out.

Implementation

The button for converting a normal table into an Excel table is located on the "Insert" ribbon:

1. Select your data.
2. Go to the "Insert" ribbon.
3. Click on "Table" within the "Tables" group on the left-hand side.
4. Check if the settings related to the data location and headers are correct. Confirm with "OK."

---

[19] In this case, we're concerned with the structured table format in Excel and not the data tables, which are part of the "What-If" analysis functions on the "Data" ribbon. For the analysis function (which is also called a data table), please refer to page 39.

A faster way to do this is to just select any cell within your data-cell range and press Ctrl + T on the keyboard.

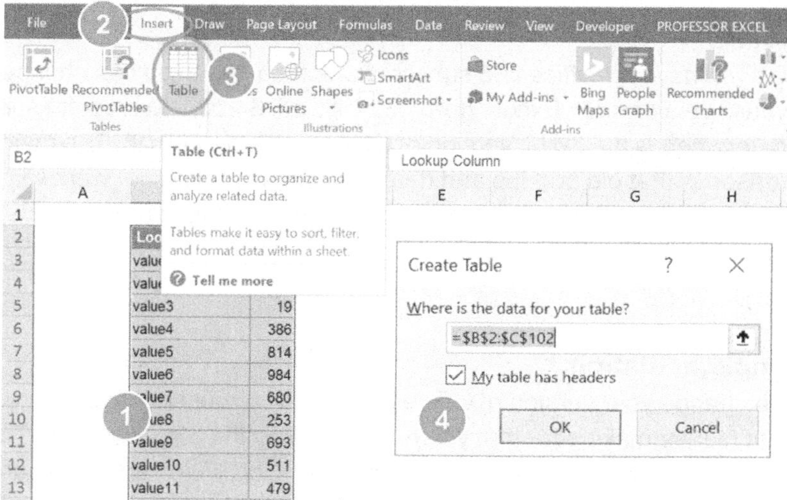

Figure 31: Converting a normal cell range into an Excel table

Impact

A test that used 100,000 VLOOKUP formulas on a cell range with 10,000 rows showed only minor improvement: the calculation time was reduced by just 1 percent.

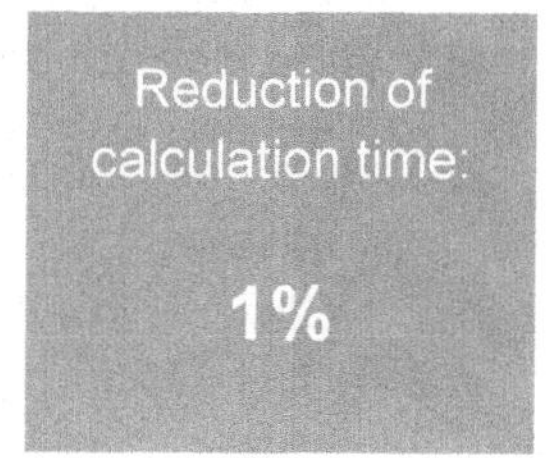

Recommendation: Unless you want to use the Excel table format for another reason anyway, then it's probably not worth spending the effort to implement this format.

16. Install the 64-bit version of Excel

Idea

Do you have an Office 365 subscription? If so, then you can change your version of Excel from 32-bit to 64-bit. Microsoft still recommends the 32-bit version of Office as the default (9). The main reason is that old add-ins and data connections might not work with 64-bit.[20] There is one condition (of course): your computer must support 64-bit software.

Implementation

To change your version of Office to 64-bit, you must reinstall Office. But please make sure that you're still running the 32-bit version. To check your Microsoft Office version, click on "File" and then on "Account" on the left-hand side. Click on the large "About Excel" button on the right-hand side. If "64-bit" appears at the end of the green headline of the new window, then you can skip this method.

Reinstalling the 64-bit version of Excel can be done on the office.com website. The process is shown in figure 32. Please note that the steps might change on the office.com website over time.

1. Go to office.com and log in with your username and password.
2. Click on the "Install Office" button.
3. Click on "Language, 32/64-bit, and other install options."
4. Select "Office—64-bit" in the version list box.
5. Confirm with "Install."

---

[20] For the detailed advantages and disadvantages, please refer to http://bit.ly/Office64vs32Bit. (Or, the full internet address is: https://support.office.com/en-us/article/Choose-between-the-64-bit-or-32-bit-version-of-Office-2dee7807-8f95-4d0c-b5fe-6c6f49b8d261)

6. Follow the steps shown on the screen.

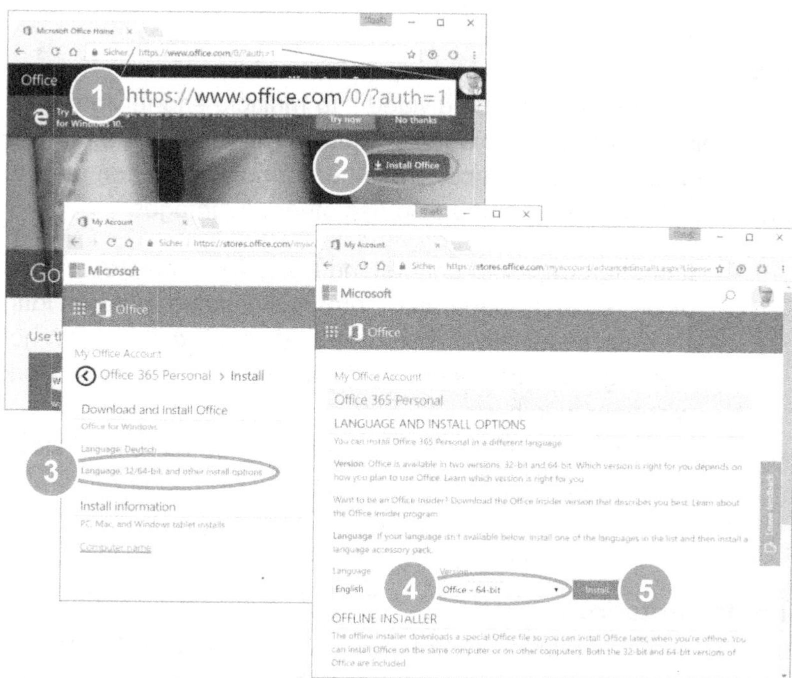

Figure 32: Installing the 64-bit version of Office

Impact

A test on a workbook with 100,000 VLOOKUP formulas showed a reduced calculation time of 9 percent.

Recommendation: Although these steps do require some effort, it is usually worth spending the time to do them, because you only need to go through the steps once.

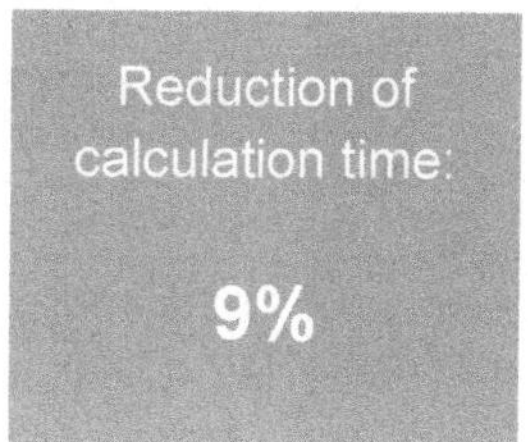

17. Divide formulas into separate cells

Idea

Some long formulas can be divided into multiple shorter formulas. The main advantage of doing this is that some parts of the formula must only be calculated once, and other formulas can then refer to that calculation. This method also has other advantages.

- It is often easier to understand the calculation steps when using shorter, separated formulas instead of one long formula, especially if you've opened your Excel file after not working on it for a while or if somebody else tries to work with your workbook.
- You can replace the formulas of some of the "small" steps with values, as described in method 27 on page 97.

Implementation

The application of this method is again very individual. You should try to find any recurring calculations and separate them into different cells.

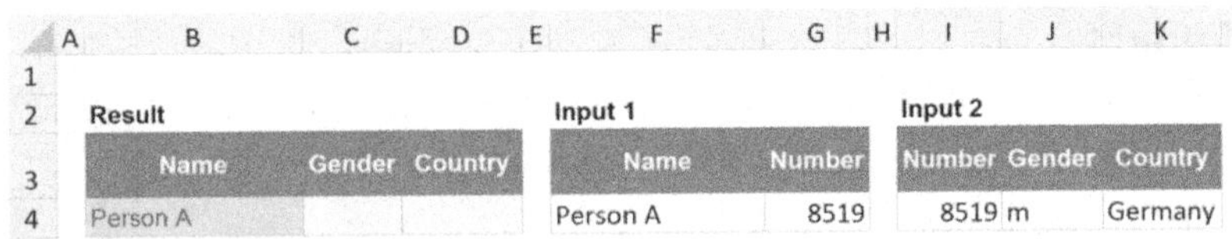

Figure 33: The starting point of an example for separating one long formula into two cells

Figure 33 above shows the starting point of an example. Say you have two input tables and one result table. You want to get the gender and country from input 2 into cells C4 and D4. You have a name in cell B4. Input 1 translates the name into a number, and input 2 provides the information identified by the number.

Figure 34 illustrates the calculation steps. For the person's name, do a lookup for the number. Next, do a second lookup with the number in input table 2 for finding the gender, which should be returned to cell C4. You can achieve both steps with just one long formula, for example `=VLOOKUP(VLOOKUP(B4,F:G,2,FALSE),I:K,2,FALSE)`.

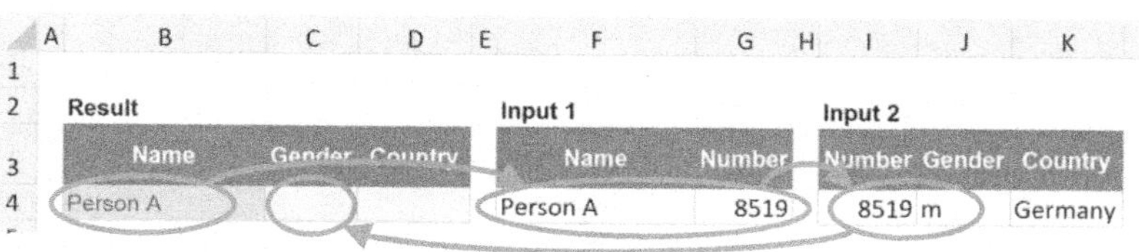

Figure 34: Calculation steps for a double lookup

Repeat the same steps with the country in cell D4. In both cells, you will first perform a lookup for the number. It is unnecessary to perform this lookup for the number twice; the formula can be separated into a single new cell.

	Name	Number	Gender	Country		Name	Number		Number	Gender	Country
Result					Input 1			Input 2			
	Person A	8519	m	Germany		Person A	8519		8519	m	Germany

Figure 35: One possible solution is to separate the number (which is required for cells D4 and E4) shown in cell C4

As you can see in figure 35, the number is now in a separate column (cell C4 in this case). Cells D4 and E4 both refer to cell C4 to get the corresponding information from input 2.

Impact

The impact again will depend on your specific workbook. The example above showed a reduced calculation time of 13 percent.

Reduction of calculation time:

13%

18. Delete unused content

Idea

Often during the process of setting up a workbook, you'll gather worksheets and cells that you no longer need. This additional content might slow down the calculation process.

Implementation

Walk through the workbook and check to see which content you no longer need. Delete it if possible.

Here's some advice on deleting content in Excel.

- If possible, delete complete worksheets. Also, removing pure data sheets (without any formulas) can make Excel calculate faster. As a rule of thumb, the more formulas a worksheet uses, the slower Excel gets.
- Delete complete worksheets by right-clicking on the sheet tab (the sheet name on the bottom of the window) and then clicking on "Delete" (see number 1 in figure 36). Using the keyboard shortcut Alt → H → D → S (press the keys sequentially), you can delete the currently active worksheet.
- Even if you can't delete entire worksheets, you can still delete parts of them.
  - Select entire rows or columns, and press the two keys Ctrl + "-" (minus) simultaneously on the keyboard to remove the selected rows.
  - If you only want to delete a few cells, select them and click on the "Clear" button on the right-hand side of the "Home" ribbon; it looks like a small eraser. Next, click on "Clear All" (see number 2 in figure 36). This will also delete the formatting.

- Please consider saving backup copies of your workbook, in case you have to delete any important content.

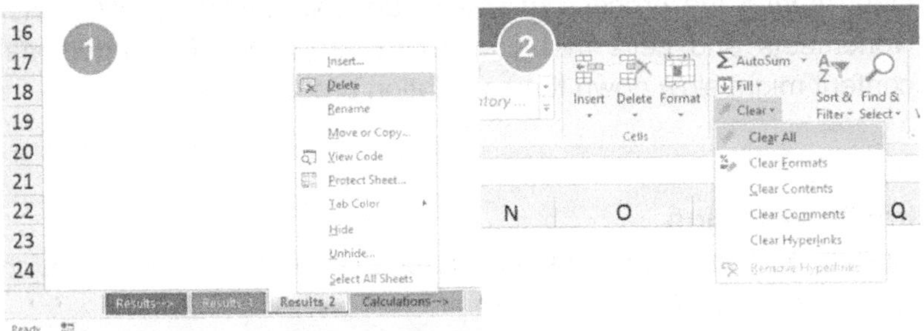

Figure 36: Deleting complete worksheets (1) or clearing cells (2) to speed up Excel

Impact

This method yielded a significant difference in performance during testing. Calculating the same number of formulas in a large file appeared to be slower than was the case with a smaller Excel file.

Reduction of calculation time:

8%

A test that used a fairly unusual workbook (in terms of unused worksheets[21]) showed a reduced calculation time of 8 percent after removing unused data from the file. The actual number, of course, will depend on the amount of data you have in your file.

---

[21] The large test file had 26 worksheets and had a file size of 26,116 KB, whereas the small test file contained a single worksheet and was only 2,336 KB in size. The deleted data didn't contain any formulas; it only contained "hard" values.

19. Disable Excel add-ins

Idea

Excel add-ins provide helpful additional features, although some add-ins might use system resources or (in some cases) may lead to longer calculation times. For example, not-optimized user-defined formulas might slow down the calculations in Excel.

Implementation

Follow these steps to deactivate add-ins in Excel.

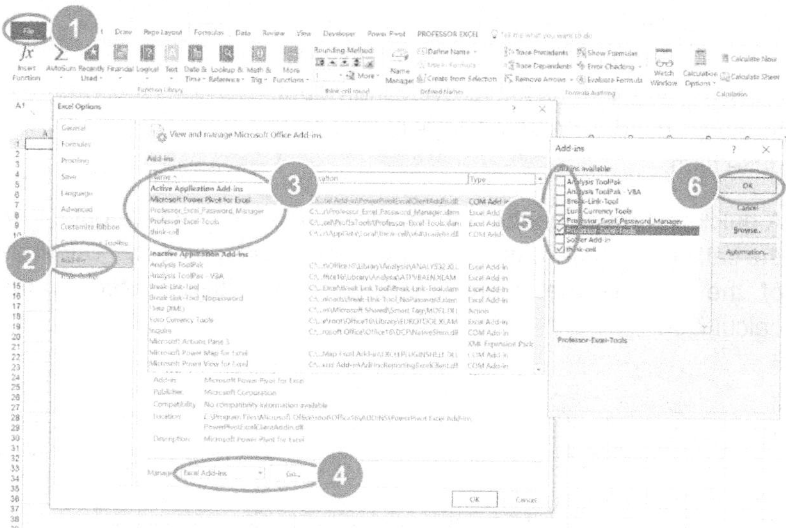

Figure 37: Disabling Excel add-ins to speed up Excel

1. Go to "File" and click on "Options" on the left-hand side.

2. Click on "Add-ins" on the left.
3. Look at the enabled add-ins. If no active add-ins are listed, then you can stop here.
4. Disable any active add-ins by selecting, for example, "COM add-Ins." Then click on "Go."
5. Uncheck any add-ins that you don't necessarily need. You can still enable them later if you need them again.
6. Confirm with "OK."

Impact

The effect of disabling all Excel add-ins highly depends on the add-ins you use. For many add-ins—those that aren't triggered when calculating something—you won't see any improvement. The impact of disabling any add-ins that provide individual formulas used in your workbook could be quite high.

Reduction of calculation time:

1%

A quick test revealed that the impact of this method was quite low: the calculation time was reduced by less than 1 percent.[22] But none of the add-ins that were enabled were actively used in the calculation.

---

[22] Tested with the following Excel add-ins enabled: *Analysis ToolPak*, *Analysis ToolPak—VBA*, *Euro Currency Tools*, *Professor_Excel_Password_Manager*, *Professor-Excel-Tools*, *Solver Add-in*, and *think-cell*.

20. Close any other background programs

Idea

The obvious step is to close any programs running in the background that unnecessarily consume system resources. These can be internet browsers, music programs, or other Microsoft Office programs, among other things. You should also check which programs are running in the background.

Implementation

Open the Task Manager and check which programs are running. To achieve this, right-click on the taskbar (the bar on the bottom of the screen). Click on "Task Manager." Now you'll see the window shown in figure 38. This shows the apps that are running as well as their usage of your computer's resources (CPU, memory, and the like). You can close programs by right-clicking on them and then clicking on "End task." Please make sure that you've saved your work in these programs. A better way would be to open any apps you want to close and then close them from within the respective programs.

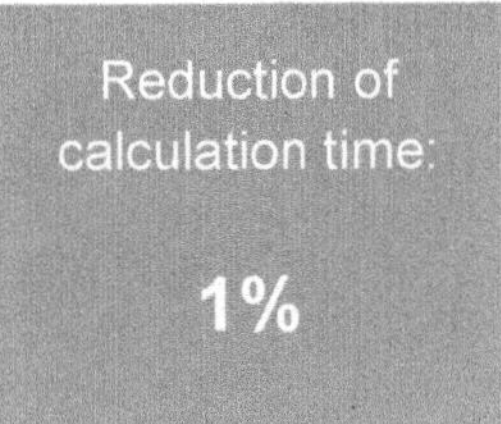

Figure 38: Viewing and closing background programs using the Task Manager

Impact

The effect will strongly depend on the programs you have running. Removing a few basic Microsoft Office programs will reduce the calculation time by around 1 percent.

Reduction of calculation time:

1%

21. Use a faster computer

Idea

This is a simple concept: faster computers allow faster calculations. Of course, because buying or renting a computer is often expensive, you should consider if the effect of a faster computer will be worth the price.

Implementation

No specific steps are required for this method other than buying or renting a faster computer, but there are alternatives to actually buying new hardware: virtual computers. A few providers (for example Microsoft) offer virtual computers.[23] These kinds of virtual machines are usually paid for by the time you use them and have adjusted them to your desired configurations.

Impact

As is so often the case, the impact will depend on both your "old" and your "new" computer. A test using a 2013 MacBook Pro[24] running Windows (medium configuration) via Bootcamp and a 2016 Lenovo ThinkPad (better configuration) showed a 7 percent reduction of calculation time in the latter.

Reduction of calculation time:

7%

---

[23] For more information about the virtual machines Microsoft offers, please refer to https://azure.microsoft.com/en-us/trial/free-trial-virtual-machines/.

[24] MacBook Pro: Intel Core i5, 2.4 GHz, 8.00 GB RAM; Lenovo ThinkPad: Intel Core i7-6500U CPU, 2.50 GHz, 8.00 GB RAM.

22. Avoid conditional formatting

Idea

Formatting is not necessary for calculations. It's just formatting. Of course, your file should look professional and respectable, but if you're suffering from long calculation times, then you should try to avoid conditional formatting, especially if you're using formulas within your conditional-formatting rules, because these formulas also need to be calculated.

Implementation

The first option is to remove conditional-formatting rules. The steps are shown in figure 39.

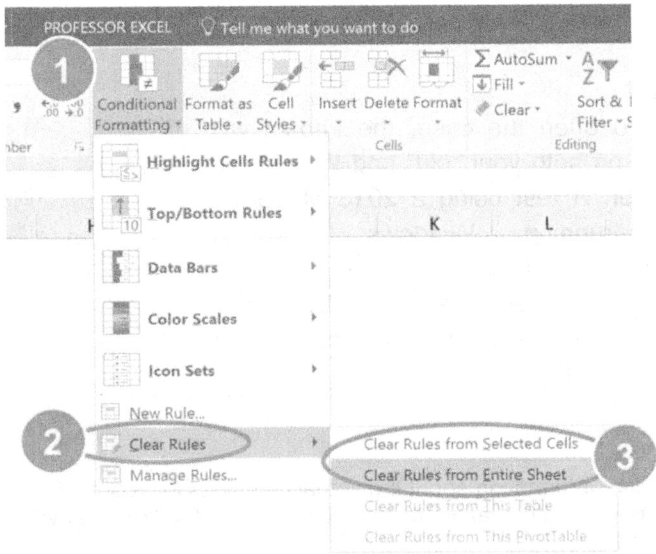

Figure 39: Removing conditional-formatting rules

Impact

As in many other cases, the impact of this method will depend on your workbook. You have to differentiate between standard conditional formatting (using the standard built-in rules) and advanced rules, such as formulas. In Excel, you can use formulas for conditional-formatting rules. Please keep in mind that these formulas will also be recalculated and because of that may slow down the calculation process.

Reduction of calculation time: 1%

A test revealed that removing a few standard conditional-formatting rules[25] only led to a performance improvement of 1 percent.

---

[25] The test was conducted on a large number of cells using standard conditional-formatting rules, highlighting any duplicates and highlighting any values smaller than a defined number.

23. Avoid or delete defined names

Idea

Defined names are a great feature in Excel. You can give a name to a cell or cell range; then, in your formulas, you can easily refer to that name instead of to the cell address. But that's not all: defined names can also contain formulas and can therefore become dynamic.

The problem is that defined names need to be recalculated. If you avoid defined names, then you can reduce the calculation time, because you reduce the complexity of the calculation process.

Implementation

Removing names from cells or cell ranges requires two steps: deleting the name and repairing any broken formulas.

Step 1: Delete the defined name.

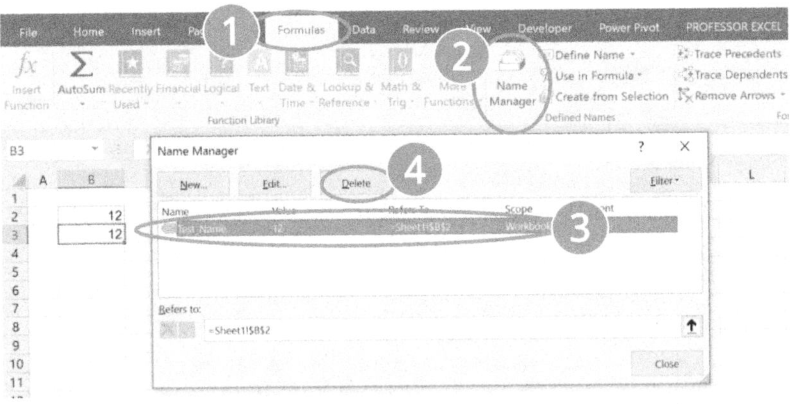

Figure 40: Steps for deleting defined names

1. Go to the "Formulas" ribbon.

2. Click on "Name Manager."
3. Select the name or names you'd like to remove.
4. Click on "Delete."

Step 2: Repair any broken formulas.

Unfortunately, because your formulas still use the defined names as cell references, you now must replace the defined names with the cell addresses. This step takes some time, because you have to repair each formula individually.

Here's an example. The name "Test_Name" refers to Sheet1!$B$2. In cell B3, the formula `=Test_Name` uses that name. After deleting the defined name (according to figure 40), the formula in cell B3 still says `=Test_Name` but, because the name no longer exists, it returns a "#NAME?" error. You should now enter the cell and type `=B2` (or use the full address `=Sheet1!$B$2`).

Impact

The impact of deleting or avoiding defined names depends on the names you use. A test workbook that included only direct references as names resulted in a performance improvement of 1 percent. But if you have formulas within your defined names, then the increased calculation speeds can be much higher.

24. Optimize your computer "for best performance"

Idea

One presumably good idea is to make the whole computer run faster. You should optimize your computer whenever and wherever possible.

Windows provides the function to adjust the computer "for best performance." This has only one downside: especially on Windows 7, the desktop and menus will look 15 years older. With Windows 10 or Windows 8, the look and feel might suffer a little bit, but the menus and fonts will not look as bad as they will with Windows 7.

Implementation

Note: before you start to apply the following steps, please have a look at the expected impact on page 93.

Several steps are necessary to navigate to the computer's performance options.

1. Open the Control Panel and click on "System." If your Control Panel is organized by category, then click on "System and Security" (the first button) and then on "System."
2. On the left-hand side, click on "Advanced system settings."
3. Go to the "Advanced" tab.
4. Click on "Settings" within the performance group.
5. Select "Adjust for best performance."

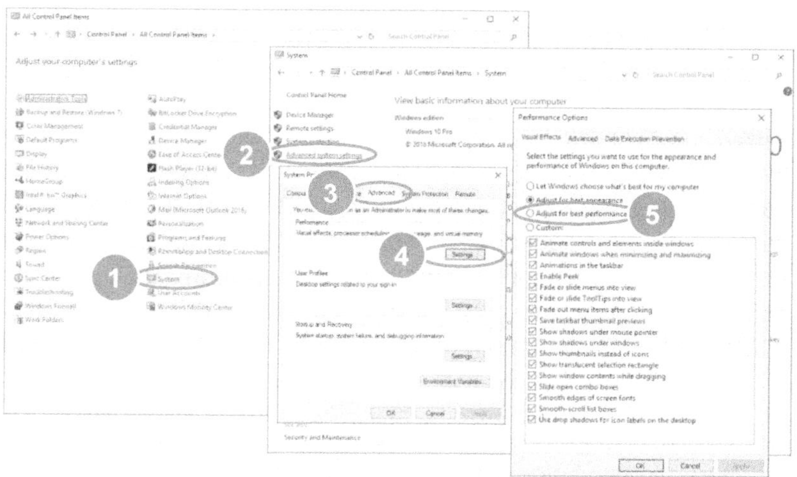

Figure 41: Adjusting the computer "for best performance"

Impact

Under different settings and on two different computers, the impact of this method was not measurable: Excel required the same time for a full calculation with each one.

Recommendation: Although this may yield tiny improvements in calculation performance, in many cases the visual compromises from using this method will not make it worthwhile.

Reduction of calculation time:

0%

25. Move data into one worksheet

Idea

One piece of advice you'll sometimes find on the internet for speeding up Excel is to move as much content onto one Excel sheet as possible. The alleged reason for this is that if the calculations are spread over too many worksheets, Excel's performance might suffer. For example, for lookup formulas (VLOOKUP and INDEX/MATCH, for example), keeping the data and lookup formulas on the same worksheet could speed up calculations.

On the other hand, the use of several worksheets provides a clear structure of the whole workbook.

Implementation

The application of this method is easy: just move your lookup formulas to the sheet with the lookup data, which you can do by cutting the cells (Ctrl + X on the keyboard) and pasting them into the data sheet.

Impact

A simple test revealed that the reduction of calculation time was insignificant at best. Worse still, the test calculation actually took slightly longer when the data and formulas were on the same sheet.

Recommendation: Skip this method.

Reduction of calculation time:

-0.3%

26. Switch Excel to manual-calculation mode

Idea

By default, Excel instantly calculates each change you make. This behavior can make your workbook performance quite slow, especially for large workbooks that contain sophisticated formulas. Instead of letting Excel permanently calculate all changes and their dependent cells, you can switch Excel to the manual-calculation mode and only let Excel perform calculations when you actively initiate the calculation.

For more information on the manual-calculation mode, please refer to the "Calculation modes" starting on page 15.

Implementation

Switching to the manual-calculation mode is very simple:

1. Go to the "Formulas" ribbon.
2. Click on "Calculation Options" on the right-hand side.
3. Select "Manual."

Please keep in mind that the manual-calculation mode can lead to some confusion because Excel doesn't permanently display the correct results; instead, Excel only recalculates when you press F9. Please refer to page 20 for an overview of the options available for initiating a calculation.

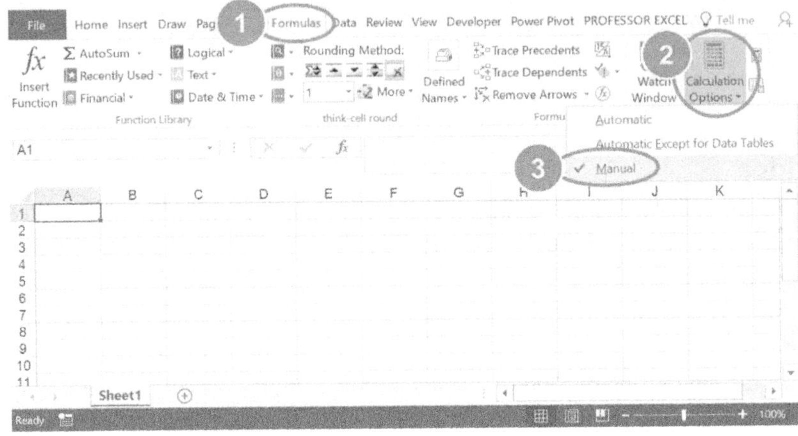

Figure 42: Switching Excel to manual-calculation mode

Impact

The impact of using manual mode for automatic calculation is highly dependent on your choice of when to initiate a calculation. A full calculation will not show any performance improvement, however.

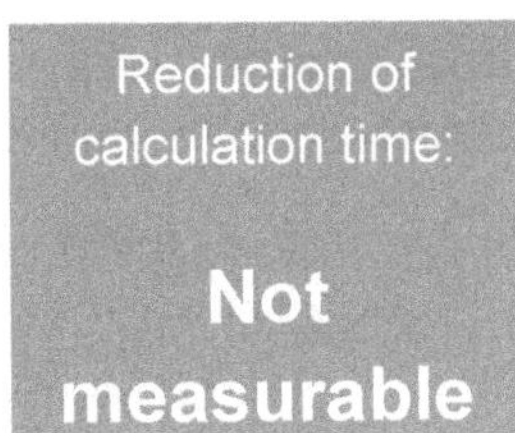

27. Replace formulas with values

Idea

If you have formulas in your Excel workbook that you won't be changing in the future, you can replace them with values to increase the speed. For example, say you have input data and you're doing some initial modifications or calculations; based on these calculations, you then conduct further analyses. You can replace these initial formulas with values.

Recommendation: Save the formula once somewhere so that you'll still be able to update it if necessary.

Implementation

The process of converting formulas to values in Excel is simple.

1. First, select the cell range that contains formulas. Copy the cell range by pressing Ctrl + C on the keyboard.
2. Then, instead of simply pasting the copied cells, use the "Paste special" function. To do this, press Ctrl + Alt + V on the keyboard.
3. Next, select the values. This is the third entry on the left-hand side of the "Paste Special" window.
4. Confirm with "OK."

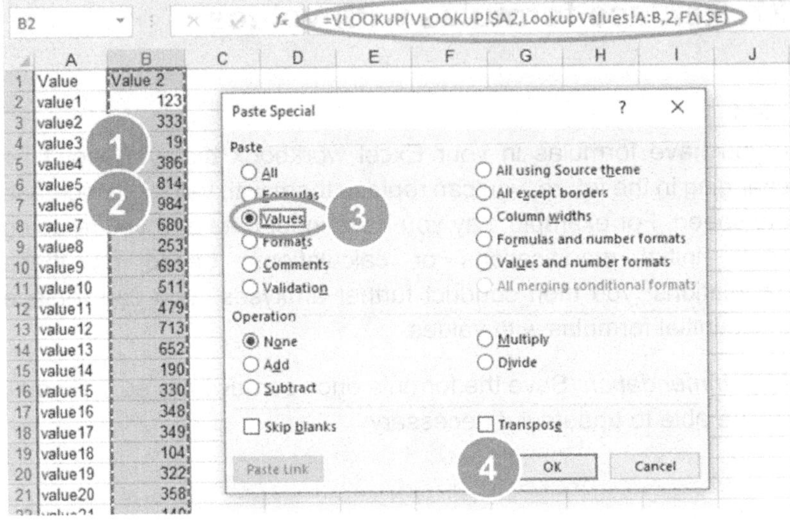

Figure 43: Steps for converting formulas to values

Impact

The impact of this method highly depends on which formulas you convert to values. If you replace calculation-intensive formulas with values, then you'll see a significant impact.

On the other hand, if the replaced formulas are not within an uncalculated part of the calculation chain (please refer to page 13 for more information), you won't experience any improvements.

Reduction of calculation time:

Not measurable

28. Avoid volatile formulas

Idea

Volatile formulas are calculated every time Excel calculates, regardless of whether you've made changes to these formulas or their predecessors. The following formulas are volatile:

- NOW
- TODAY
- RAND
- OFFSET
- INDIRECT
- INFO (depending on its arguments)
- CELL (depending on its arguments)

Please refer to page 12 for more information on volatile formulas.

Implementation

Because these formulas—especially INDIRECT and OFFSET—are very powerful, you should consider whether you can replace or omit them.

Different alternatives do exist to the volatile functions listed above. The easiest way is to replace the formulas with values, as described on page 97. The disadvantage of this method is that your workbook might lose its dynamism.

Probably the most frequently used volatile formulas are INDIRECT and OFFSET. These two formulas don't have any exact alternatives, but you can try to set up a workaround.

- First, reorganize your data. If INDIRECT switches between worksheets, then you might consider merging your data into one worksheet.
- You could replace OFFSET with a SUMIFS formula and helper columns, or perhaps the INDEX formula.

The actual method you use will depend on your situation, since there is no universal solution.

Impact

This method's impact on your calculation speed will depend on your usage of the volatile formulas listed above. If you can replace them with nonvolatile formulas, then Excel will not recalculate them unless a preceding cell has changed.

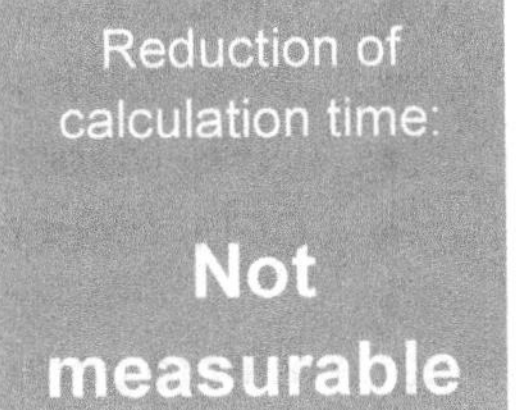

29. Divide the workbook into several small files

Idea

Large Excel workbooks often contain several calculation steps. For example, these might include

1. handling and processing the raw data;
2. making any iterations and consolidations in a second step;
3. creating final outputs (e.g., deriving conclusions, tables, and charts).

You can divide each of these steps into a separate workbook so that the calculations that are performed for each step are much smaller.

Implementation

Let's assume the following situation. You've received a large amount of raw data, for example of 100,000 rows and 100 columns. You need to use this output from an ERP system as the starting point for your calculations.

The first step is to import the data into Excel. Now you can do some matching, filtering, and the like. For example, you can use the "Filter" function in Excel to reduce the number of rows to the 20,000 rows you actually need. You can also delete 80 columns. The data you'll need for your analysis will then just be 20,000 rows by 20 columns. Copy this cell range into a new workbook.

Now you can do your analysis using only the reduced amount of data.

Impact

The impact of this method again depends fully on your file and how well you can divide your workbook.

Reduction of calculation time:

Not measurable

30. Use PowerPivot for large data sets

Idea

Roughly speaking, PowerPivot offers a way to use a PivotTable on very large data sets. PowerPivot jumps in when normal PivotTables reach their limits. It provides a good opportunity to consolidate your data before further analyzing it using normal Excel functions.

Implementation

If you have Excel 2013 or 2016 ProPlus, then PowerPivot is already built in.[26] If you can't see the "PowerPivot" ribbon, please activate it within the Options. Follow the steps below, or refer to page 83 for a detailed description with screenshots.

1. Go to "File" and click on "Options" on the left-hand side.
2. Click on "Add-ins."
3. Because PowerPivot is a COM add-in, select "COM add-ins" and click "Go."
4. Check the box "Microsoft PowerPivot for Excel" and confirm with "OK."

If you have Excel 2010 or older, then you can download PowerPivot from the Microsoft website for free: go to the website, select your

---

[26] Unfortunately, which versions of Excel or Office include PowerPivot is quite obscure. For Excel 2016, the following versions come with PowerPivot: Office 365 ProPlus, Office 365 E3, Office 365 E4 and E5, and Excel 2016 standalone. The following versions do *not* have PowerPivot: Home and Business, Home and Student, Office 365 Home, Office 365 Personal, Office 365 Business Essentials, Office 365 Business, Office 365 Business Premium, and Office 365 Enterprise E1 (11). Because the features that are included in each package and version of Excel change over time, please conduct your own research to make sure that you can still use PowerPivot.

language, and click "Download."[27] If you have the 64-bit version of Excel, then you should download the link with "64" in it. If you have the 32-bit version, then you must choose the file with "x86" in it.

Using PowerPivot is quite straightforward. Just follow these steps:

1. Start by clicking "Manage" on the "PowerPivot" ribbon.
2. Click on "Get External Data."
3. In addition to database formats (as well as Microsoft Access, which can be useful), you can also import text files or other Excel files. In this case, you'll use another Excel file.
4. Locate the file on your drive and follow the steps on the screen for the import process. Please note that the import will take some time for large amounts of data. It might look as if Excel has crashed, but in most cases, it has not. After some time has passed, the screen will display the number of rows that have already been imported.
5. When the import is finished, you can see the data in the main PowerPivot window. To create a PivotTable from the data, click on "PivotTable." Next, select the place to create the PivotTable.

---

[27] The current version of PowerPivot for Office 2010 can be found here: https://www.microsoft.com/en-us/download/details.aspx?id=29074.

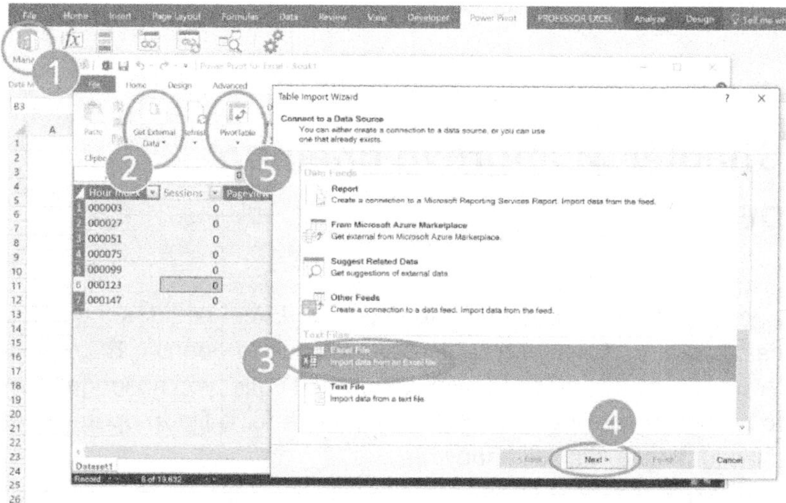

Figure 44: Steps for using PowerPivot in Excel

Now you can drag and drop the data as in normal PivotTables.

Impact

The PowerPivot Excel add-in does not make your computer calculate faster. It is an option to avoid calculations and formulas. Therefore, the impact will depend on any formulas (and normal PivotTables) that you can replace.

PowerPivot is also a way of handling large amounts of data. While PivotTables and formulas often time out with a few hundred thousand rows of data, PowerPivot can handle millions of rows of data.

Chapter 3: Improve opening performance

Another important aspect of speeding up Excel besides the actual calculation performance is the performance of opening Excel files. You might object that once you've opened a file, you no longer want to be bothered. But waiting for one minute for a file to open—even if it's just once—is still annoying.

This chapter introduces five simple methods that speed up the process of opening Excel files. As we did previously, each method is outlined by the three "I"s: idea, implementation, and impact. As before, the impact is measured with a simple VBA macro designed for a test workbook. Although the actual effects you'll experience might differ according to your own situation, the numbers should provide a rough idea of what to expect when you apply these methods.

01. The XLSB file type

Idea

The XLSB file type was designed to keep file sizes and load times low. The file format is a binary format, which means the source code of your Excel file can only be read by computers, not by humans. In addition, other Office programs might experience problems opening them. Please refer to page 59 for more information on the XLSB file format.

Implementation

This is one of the easiest methods of reducing the load time of Excel workbooks. You can save your Excel file in XLSB file format by going to "File" and clicking on "Save as." Alternatively, press F12 on the keyboard to open the "Save as" window. Choose the file format XLSB in the lower part of the "Save as" window, as shown in figure 23 on page 61.

Impact

Again, the impact will depend on your file. Most importantly, the impact will depend on the original file size in the XLSX format.

Figure 45 shows the relationship between the size of an XLSX file and opening times (in the solid line). The dotted line indicates the opening times if you change the XLSX file to XLSB. When you change the file type, the size of the Excel file decreases. The dotted line shows the speed of the corresponding XLSX file for comparison.

As you can see in figure 45, the opening time for a 5 MB XLSX file took approximately 3.0 seconds. After changing the file type to XLSB (the file size reduced to 3.5 MB), the opening time was reduced to 1.5 seconds. That's a reduction of 50 percent, but in terms of absolute number, it's "just" 1.5 seconds.

With a 10 MB workbook, the opening time decreased from 5.4 to 2.5 seconds; the reduction in this case was 54 percent, or 2.9 seconds. At the same time, you've shrunk the file size from 10 MB to 5 MB.

With a file size of 78 MB, switching the file type from XLSX to XLSB will reduce the file size to 55 MB, and the time for opening the file will change from 46 seconds to 14 seconds. You save 69 percent of the time, or 32 seconds.

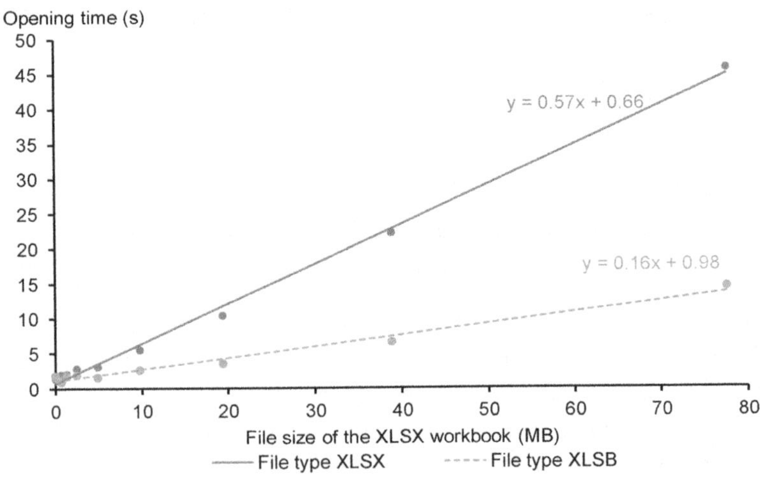

Figure 45: Opening times for an Excel workbook in the XLSX and XLSB formats

Recommendation: Because the XLSB file format comes with a few disadvantages (see page 60), you should only use the XLSB format when it's worth it; this is usually the case when the file size exceeds 10 MB.

02. Disable synchronization clients

Idea

Synchronization clients such as Dropbox, OneDrive, Google Drive, and so on constantly track files and their changes. If you quit a synchronization client such as OneDrive, then opening Excel files should be faster.

Implementation

You have two choices here: either temporarily close the synchronization client, or do so permanently. The following steps describe Microsoft OneDrive, but they also work for other sync clients.

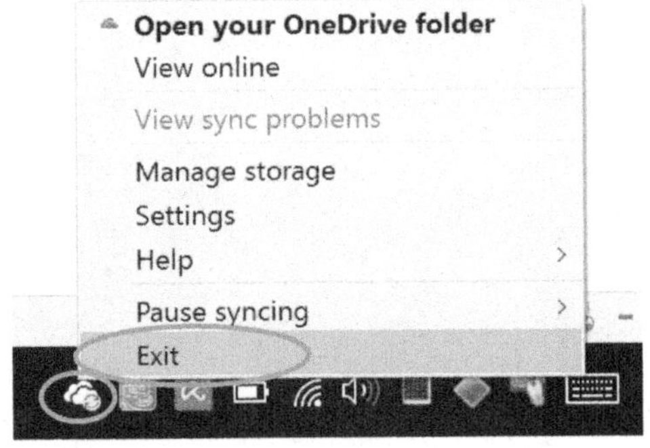

Figure 46: Closing synchronization clients to reduce opening times

Here are the steps to temporarily disable OneDrive.

1.   Right-click on the OneDrive icon in the task bar.

2. Click on "Exit" and confirm your choice by clicking on the "Close OneDrive" button.

If you want to disable OneDrive permanently, you can either uninstall it (right-click on the Start icon, click on "Programs and Features," select "Microsoft OneDrive," and click on "Uninstall"), or you can just disable the "AutoStart" function so that you'll still occasionally be able to start it manually if you so desire. To do this, follow the steps shown in figure 47.

1. Right-click on the task bar and click on "Task Manager."
2. Go to the "Startup" tab.
3. Right-click on "Microsoft OneDrive."
4. Click on "Disable."

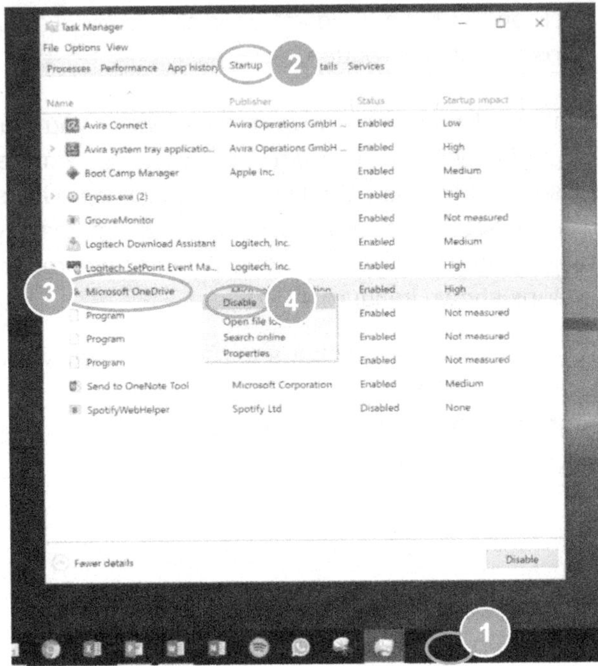

Figure 47: Alternatively, you can disable synchronization clients during the startup process

Impact

The impact of disabling the OneDrive client is quite high: the test file loaded 46 percent faster than before OneDrive was disabled.

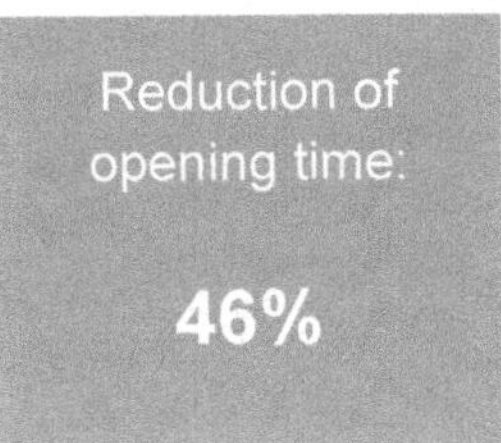

03. Replace formulas with values

Idea

When Excel loads an Excel file, it not only opens the data but also builds the initial calculation chain. And, if Excel is set to automatic-calculation mode, then it will recalculate all uncalculated cells, all volatile functions, and all depending cells. Another effect is that for formulas, Excel stores the calculated values as well as the formula, meaning that formulas also increase the file size.

If you reduce the number of formulas in your workbook and replace them with values, then you should be able to reduce the opening times of your Excel workbook.

Implementation

For parts of your Excel workbook that don't require frequent recalculation, you can copy the formulas and paste them as values. You should save the underlying formula in a highlighted cell first. That way, it will still be easy to do updates on the values if some of the input cells change. This process is described in detail on page 97.

Impact

Unfortunately, the impact will depend on how many and which formulas you can replace. In general, lookup and array formulas will have a bigger impact than (for example) simple sums. As a test, 100,000 VLOOKUP formulas were replaced with values, and the opening time of the Excel file was reduced by 18 percent.

04. Disable Excel add-ins

Idea

Many people use add-ins in Excel. Add-ins extend the functionality of Excel, often by doing specialized tasks. Unfortunately, depending on your Excel add-ins, they might run certain procedures on your workbook when you open it, which will slow down the opening process.

Implementation

Please refer to page 83 for a detailed description of the steps for disabling add-ins. Here's a summary. Click on "File" and then on "Options" on the left pane. In the new window, click on "Add-ins." Now you can see all active add-ins in the upper part of the window. Select "Excel Add-ins" or "COM Add-ins," depending on the type of the add-ins you want to disable. Click the "Go" button. Now you can remove the check marks of any add-ins to disable them.

Impact

To test the impact, seven add-ins (a few built-in add-ons and a few external add-ins) were enabled and disabled. The opening time during testing was reduced by 12 percent, although the time reduction for opening your Excel workbook will depend on the particular add-ins you use.

Reduction of opening time:

12%

05. Reduce the file size of your Excel file

Idea

The larger the file size, the more data must be loaded into the memory; the more data to be loaded, the more time it takes. The idea here is to keep the Excel file small and remove any unnecessary data.

Implementation

Go through your Excel file and delete everything you don't need for your actual calculations. In the process of creating your Excel file, it's very common to accumulate outdated or unnecessary data.

Please refer to page 81 for more information on deleting unused contents, and to page 101 for information on dividing your large Excel file into several smaller files.

Impact

File size has a direct impact on the opening time of an Excel file. For each additional MB, the test workbook required 0.57 seconds longer to open. This means that you can easily reduce the opening times of your Excel files by decreasing their file sizes. Figure 48 shows this relationship.

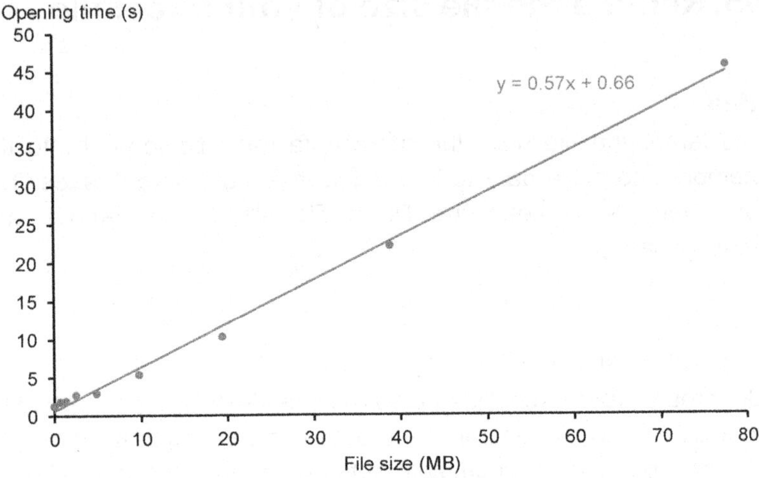

Figure 48: Opening times directly depend on Excel file sizes

Conclusion

Excel often takes a long time to calculate a workbook, especially with large Excel files. The reasons for this are different for each workbook. Because of that some methods for speeding up Excel might work well, and some will not. Some methods work in general for all workbooks, while others will only work if your workbook meets certain criteria. As a rough guideline, I recommend the following approach.

Step 1: Undertake general and permanent improvements that will have a significant impact first.

- Set your computer to manual-calculation mode instead of automatic mode; this will give you full control of when and what to calculate (please refer to pages 15 and 95).
- Use all available processors for calculations (see page 29).
- Switch your computer's region to "English (United States)." Please refer to page 34 for more information.
- Get the 64-bit version of Excel (page 76).
- Set the "realtime" priority for Excel in the Windows Task Manager, as described on page 72. You must do this every single time you start Excel again.[28]
- Upgrade your hardware, either through a virtual machine or with a faster computer (page 87).

---

[28] Please be aware that Windows warns you that your computer might become unstable when you change the priority of a task.

Step 2: Apply various specialized methods, depending on your Excel workbook. If your answer to any of the following questions is no, then that criterion does not apply to your Excel workbook; in that case, you can just move on to the next step.

- Does your file have external links? Remove the external references or keep the linked workbook open (page 26).
- Are any other workbooks open in the background? If yes, and you do not need them to be opened, then close them (page 32).
- Does your file contain data tables? Try to minimize the usage of data tables and switch Excel to the calculation mode "Automatic Except for Data Tables" (page 39).
- Does your file contain array formulas? Use either the exact cell range in array formulas (page 43) or avoid array formulas in general (page 69).
- Does your file have circular references? If yes, try to remove them or, alternatively, reduce the maximum number of iterations. Page 45 provides more information on this.
- Do your formulas refer to large "used ranges"? If yes, you should either reduce the used range to fit the actual content or adapt the cell reference in your formulas (page 49).
- Does your file have a lot of lookups? If yes, then
    - sort the lookup data (page 56);
    - use approximate lookups (page 62).
- Does your workbook have a large file size? If yes, then
    - use the XLSB file format instead of XLSX (page 59);
    - try to delete any unused content (page 81);
    - split your file into multiple smaller Excel workbooks (page 101).
- Do you use formulas within conditional-formatting rules? Try to avoid them if possible (see page 88).

- Does your workbook include formulas as defined names? Remove them to improve the calculation performance (page 90).

Step 3: Bear in mind the following general advice in your daily work.

- Use faster formulas. Many formulas in Excel have alternatives; try to use the faster option whenever possible (page 54).
- Instead of using long formulas that under some circumstances repeat the same calculation, divide the long calculation into separate cells (page 78).
- If you can, replace formulas with their calculated values. You can still save the formula in case you later want to update the values for any reason (page 97).
- Avoid volatile functions like INDIRECT or OFFSET (page 99).
- If you have a large data set within your Excel file, then a good strategy for reducing calculation times is to first summarize the data with a PivotTable or PowerPivot (page 103).

For Excel workbook opening times, many of the methods for improving calculation speeds also reduce opening times. In general, keeping the file size low is a good strategy (please refer to page 115 for more information on this). These steps will also help you to open your Excel files faster:

- Use the file type XLSB rather than XLSX (page 107).
- Disable your synchronization clients for cloud services if possible (page 110).
- Replace formulas with values (page 113).
- Disable any Excel add-ins you don't really need (page 114).

If you've done all these steps, then there's only one thing left to say: good luck. And if you're still faced with waiting times…then please have some patience!

Appendix

Overview of methods

Table 5 provides an overview of the methods introduced earlier in the book.

- The first column contains the number of the method, as listed above.
- Column 2 ("Method") shows the name of the method, as in the chapter headings.
- The third column shows the reduction in calculation times in percentages
- The fourth column shows the estimated time savings in seconds from implementing the method.
- The fifth column includes the quotient of the third and fourth column: the reduction of calculation time (in percentages per implementation second).

Please refer to figure 8 on page 24 for the chart showing the methods. The symbols in table 5 correspond to the groups in figure 8, with the following meanings.

- ↗ The reduction of calculation time is higher than 40 percent and therefore is considered "high."
- ↘ The reduction of calculation time is lower than 40 percent and therefore is considered "low."
- ✓ The application requires less than 200 seconds; the method is therefore easy to implement.
- ✗ The application requires more than 200 seconds; the method is therefore difficult to implement.

Table 5: Overview of methods for reducing calculation times

Nr.	Method	Reduction of calc. time (%)		Est. impl. time (s)		Reduction per second (%/s)
1	Avoid links to other workbooks, or keep linked workbooks open	↗	68%	✓	30	2.3%
2	Use all available processors for calculations	↗	42%	✓	20	2.1%
3	Close other workbooks in the background	↗	51%	✓	30	1.7%
4	Switch the Windows' region to "English (United States)"	↗	81%	✓	90	0.9%
5	Minimize using data tables or skip calculating data tables	↗	74%	✓	90	0.8%
6	Array formulas 1: Use the exact range in array formulas	↗	100%	✓	150	0.7%
7	Solve circular references and reduce iterations	↗	82%	✓	150	0.5%
8	Avoid large used ranges in formulas	↗	43%	✓	120	0.4%
9a	=A2+B1 vs. =SUM(A$2:A2)	↗	76%	✗	300	0.3%
10	Sort data for lookups	↘	10%	✓	45	0.2%
11	Use the XLSB file type	↘	5%	✓	30	0.2%
9b	VLOOKUP instead of SUMIFS	↗	53%	✗	300	0.2%
9c	IFERROR instead of IF(ISERROR)	↗	50%	✗	300	0.2%
12	"Approximate" and "not exact" matches in lookups	↗	99%	✗	600	0.2%
13	Array formulas 2: Avoid array formulas	↗	88%	✗	600	0.1%
14	Set "realtime" priority for Excel in the Windows Task Manager	↘	3%	✓	30	0.1%
15	Use the Excel table format for data	↘	1%	✓	20	0.1%
16	Install the 64bit version of Excel	↘	9%	✓	180	0.1%
17	Divide formulas into separate cells	↘	13%	✗	300	0.0%
9d	MAX(A1,0) instead of IF(A1>0,A1,0)	↘	6%	✗	240	0.0%
18	Delete unused content	↘	8%	✗	480	0.0%
19	Disable Excel add-ins	↘	1%	✓	60	0.0%
20	Close any other background programs	↘	1%	✓	110	0.0%
21	Use a faster computer	↘	7%	✗	700	0.0%
22	Avoid conditional formatting	↘	1%	✓	140	0.0%
23	Avoid or delete defined names	↘	1%	✗	600	0.0%
24	Optimize your computer "for best performance"	↘	0%	✓	45	0.0%
25	Move data into one worksheet	↘	0%	✓	90	0.0%
26	Switch Excel to manual manual-calculation mode		n/a	✓	20	
27	Replace formulas with values		n/a	✓	120	
28	Avoid volatile formulas		n/a	✗	300	
29	Divide the workbook into several small files		n/a	✗	300	
30	Use PowerPivot for large data sets		n/a	✗	300	

VBA macro for measuring the impact on calculation performance

If you want to measure the calculation performance of your workbook, you can use the following VBA macro to do so.[29] It creates a new worksheet in your active workbook called "Results_of_Calc_Measuring." Column A contains the start time and column B the end time of a full calculation. The actual calculation time in seconds is calculated and shown in column C.

Open the VBA editor by pressing Alt + F11 on the keyboard. Insert a new module by right-clicking on the left-hand side in the Project Explorer window, and then move the mouse to "Insert," and click on "Module." Copy the following VBA code into the new module. For your convenience, add a button to your Excel file that will start the macro. To do so, go to the "Developer"[30] ribbon and click on "Insert," and then on "Button" within the "Form Control" section. Now you can create the button on the current worksheet by clicking and dragging the shape onto the worksheet area. When you are asked which macro to assign, choose "measureCalculationTime." Each time you click the button, the VBA macro will run and record six rounds of calculation.

```
Sub measureCalculationTime()

    Dim lastRow, i, totalNumberOfRuns As Long

    'Change the number of runs here. Default is 6 with the following
    'concept: Remove the first, the slowest and fastest run.
```

---

[29] The VBA macro code is available for download at http://professor-excel.com/performance-book/

[30] If the "Developer" ribbon is not shown, then right-click on any ribbon and click "Customize the Ribbon." On the right-hand side, activate the "Developer" ribbon by checking the corresponding box.

```vba
'Use the average time of the remaining 3 runs.
totalNumberOfRuns = 6

Dim sheetName As String
sheetName = "Results_of_Calc_Measuring"

'Checking, if sheet for results exists. If not, it will be created
If Evaluate("ISREF('" & sheetName & "'!A1)") = False Then
    Sheets.Add
    ActiveSheet.Name = sheetName
    Sheets(sheetName).Cells(1, 1) = "Start time"
    Sheets(sheetName).Cells(1, 2) = "End time"
    Sheets(sheetName).Cells(1, 3) = "Time of a full calculation [s]"
End If

'Go to the results sheet
Sheets(sheetName).Activate

'Procedure for recording the calculation time
For i = 1 To totalNumberOfRuns

    'Determine the last row
    lastRow = Sheets(sheetName).Cells(20000, 1).End(xlUp).Row + 1

    'Write down the start time in column A
    Sheets(sheetName).Cells(lastRow, 1) = "=NOW()" '.Select
    Sheets(sheetName).Cells(lastRow, 1).Select
    Selection.Copy
    Selection.PasteSpecial Paste:=xlPasteValues, _
    operation:=xlNone, SkipBlanks:=False, Transpose:=False

    'Do a full calculation. If you want just a normal calculation
    'write "Application.Calculate" instead
    'of Application.CalculateFull
    Application.CalculateFull

    'Write down the end time in column B
    Sheets(sheetName).Cells(lastRow, 2) = "=NOW()"
    Sheets(sheetName).Cells(lastRow, 2).Select
    Selection.Copy
    Selection.PasteSpecial Paste:=xlPasteValues, _
        operation:=xlNone, SkipBlanks:=False, Transpose:=False

    'Calculate the time for one full calculation and write it
    'down in column C
    Sheets(sheetName).Cells(lastRow, 3) = _
        (Sheets(sheetName).Cells(lastRow, 2) _
        - Sheets(sheetName).Cells(lastRow, 1)) * 24 * 60 * 60
    Next
End Sub
```

VBA macro for measuring the impact on opening performance

The macro for measuring the opening time is very similar to the macro for measuring calculation times;[31] the only difference is that instead of running a full calculation, the macro opens and closes a file you specify. Please refer to page 123 for more information on the steps required to integrate the macro into your Excel workbook.[32]

```vba
Sub measureOpeningTime()

    Dim lastRow, i, totalNumberOfRuns As Long

    'Change the number of runs here. Default is 6 with the following
    'concept: Remove the first, the slowest and fastest run.
    'Use the average time of the remaining 3 runs.
    totalNumberOfRuns = 6

    Dim sheetName, activeWorkbookName, openWorkbookPath, _
    openWorkbookName As String
    Dim fso As New FileSystemObject

    'Copy your complete workbook path here in
    'this format "C:\Users\UserName\Desktop\ExcelFile.xlsx"
    openWorkbookPath = " C:\Users\UserName\Desktop\ExcelFile.xlsx "

    'Read the filename from the path
    openWorkbookName = fso.GetFileName(openWorkbookPath)

    sheetName = "Results_of_Open_Measuring"
```

---

[31] The VBA macro code is available for download at http://professor-excel.com/performance-book/

[32] Please note that this macro requires the Microsoft Scripting Runtime reference. If you receive the error message "Compile error: User-defined type not defined," then please check if the Microsoft Scripting Library is activated. To do so, go to "Tools" at the top of the VBA editor and click on "References." Scroll down to "Microsoft Scripting Runtime" and make sure the box is checked.

```vba
'Check, if sheet for results exists. If not, it will be created
If Evaluate("ISREF('" & sheetName & "'!A1)") = False Then
    Sheets.Add
    ActiveSheet.Name = sheetName
    Sheets(sheetName).Cells(1, 1) = "Start time"
    Sheets(sheetName).Cells(1, 2) = "End time"
    Sheets(sheetName).Cells(1, 3) = "Time of opening workbook [s]"
End If

'Go to the results sheet
Sheets(sheetName).Activate

'Store the name of the active workbook
activeWorkbookName = ActiveWorkbook.Name

'Procedure for recording the calculation time
For i = 1 To totalNumberOfRuns

    'Determine the last row
    lastRow = Sheets(sheetName).Cells(20000, 1).End(xlUp).Row + 1

    'Write down the start time in column A
    Sheets(sheetName).Cells(lastRow, 1) = "=NOW()"
    Sheets(sheetName).Cells(lastRow, 1).Select
    Selection.Copy
    Selection.PasteSpecial Paste:=xlPasteValues, _
        operation:=xlNone, SkipBlanks:=False, Transpose:=False

    Workbooks.Open fileName:=openWorkbookPath
    Windows(activeWorkbookName).Activate

    'Write down the end time in column B
    Sheets(sheetName).Cells(lastRow, 2) = "=NOW()"
    Sheets(sheetName).Cells(lastRow, 2).Select
    Selection.Copy
    Selection.PasteSpecial Paste:=xlPasteValues, _
        operation:=xlNone, SkipBlanks:=False, Transpose:=False

    'Calculate the time for one full calculation and write it
    'down in column C
    Sheets(sheetName).Cells(lastRow, 3) = _
        (Sheets(sheetName).Cells(lastRow, 2) _
        - Sheets(sheetName).Cells(lastRow, 1)) * 24 * 60 * 60

    Windows(openWorkbookName).Activate
    ActiveWorkbook.Close
    Windows(activeWorkbookName).Activate
Next
End Sub
```

Index

References

1. **Charles, Williams, Allison, Bokone and Chad, Rothschiller.** Excel 2010 Performance: Improving Calculation Performance. [Online] 4 1, 2011. [Cited: 2 26, 2017.] https://msdn.microsoft.com/en-us/library/office/ff700515%28v=office.14%29.aspx.

2. **Microsoft Corporation.** Excel recalculation. [Online] 07 01, 2011. https://msdn.microsoft.com/en-us/us-us/library/office/bb687891.aspx.

3. **Schiffner, Henrik.** Performance of Excel: Study Shows How to Speed up Excel by 81%. *Professor Excel.* [Online] November 09, 2016. [Cited: February 27, 2017.] http://professor-excel.com/performance-excel-study/.

4. **Williams, Charles, Bokone, Allison and Rothschiller, Chad.** Excel 2010 Performance: Performance and Limit Improvements. *Microsoft.* [Online] Microsoft Corporation, April 11, 2011. [Cited: February 27, 2017.] https://msdn.microsoft.com/en-us/library/office/ff700514%28v=office.14%29.aspx.

5. **Microsoft Excel Team ("Alex").** We are the Microsoft Excel Team – Ask Us Anything! *Reddit.com.* [Online] November 17, 2016. [Cited: 27 02, 2017.] https://www.reddit.com/r/IAmA/comments/5dgrf8/we_are_the_microsoft_excel_team_ask_us_anything/da4f2pq/.

6. **Schiffner, Henrik.** Region Settings: Big Impact on Excel's Calculation Speed. *Professor Excel.* [Online] December 01, 2016. [Cited: February 02, 2017.] http://professor-excel.com/region-settings/.

7. **Girvin, Mike.** *Ctrl+Shift+Enter Mastering Excel Array Formulas.* s.l. : Holy Macro! Books, 2013. 1615470077.

8. **Wikipedia.** Wikipedia. *Wikipedia.* [Online] January 4, 2017. [Cited: March 17, 2017.] https://en.wikipedia.org/wiki/Binary_file.

9. **Microsoft Corporation.** Choose between the 64-bit or 32-bit version of Office. [Online] April 09, 2017. [Cited: April 09, 2017.] https://support.office.com/en-us/article/Choose-between-the-64-bit-or-32-bit-version-of-Office-2dee7807-8f95-4d0c-b5fe-6c6f49b8d261.

10. **Wikipedia.** Thread (computing). *Wikipedia.* [Online] 2 21, 2017. [Cited: 2 27, 2017.] https://en.wikipedia.org/wiki/Thread_(computing).

11. **Collie, Rob.** What Versions of Office 2016 Contain Power Pivot? *PowerPivot Pro.* [Online] October 27, 2015. [Cited: March 30, 2017.] https://powerpivotpro.com/2015/10/what-versions-of-office-2016-contain-power-pivot/.

12. **Microsoft Corporation.** Worksheet.UsedRange Property. *Microsofto Developer Network.* [Online] [Cited: May 07, 2017.] https://msdn.microsoft.com/en-us/library/microsoft.office.tools.excel.worksheet.usedrange.aspx.

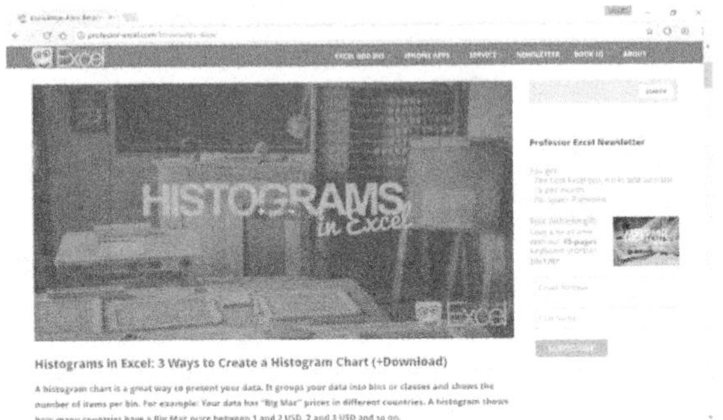

Visit **professor-excel.com**:

- A large **knowledge area**

- Great **Excel add-ins**

- Free **iPhone and iPad apps**

- Excel accessories and **gifts**

- and much more!

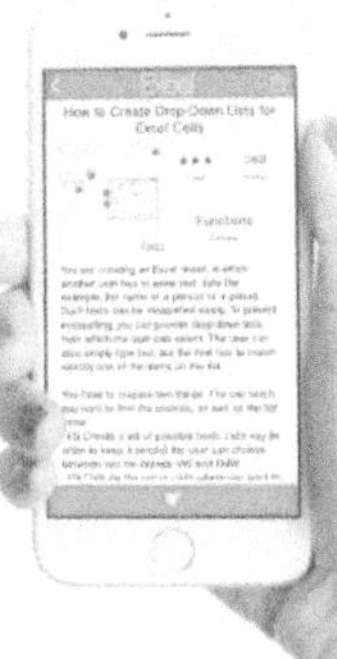

Boost your Excel knowledge and become a real Excel expert.

Sign up for the free Excel newsletter.

- 1-2x per month.
- No spam. Promised.
- Each newsletter has 2-3 Excel tips, tricks and tutorials.
- It's—of course—free!

 **professor-excel.com/newsletter**

Your welcome gift: The big keyboard shortcut guide—free.

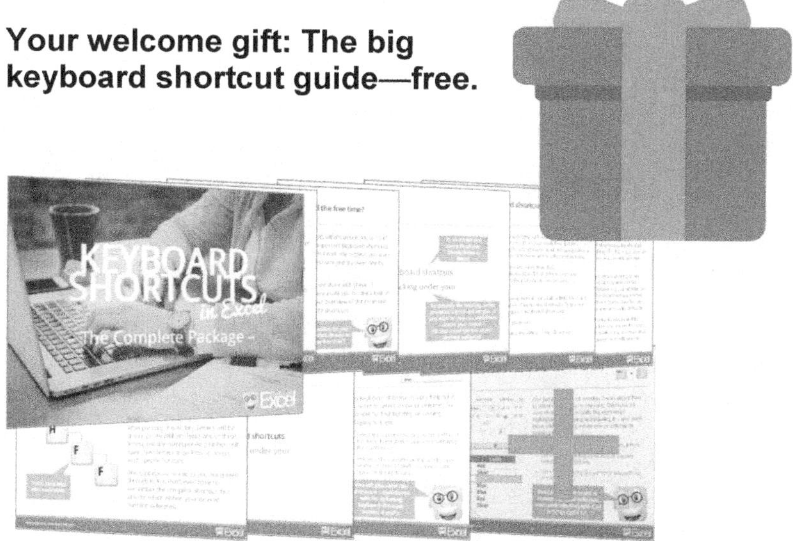

Made in the USA
Monee, IL
07 July 2026

56550373R00075